ANARCHISM
IN SPAIN

ANARCHISM IN SPAIN

CARLOS TAIBO

Translated by John Stewart

ANARRES EDITIONS

English Edition published in 2023 by Anarres Editions
an imprint of The Merlin Press
Central Books Building
Freshwater Road
London RM8 1RX
www.merlinpress.co.uk

First published in Spain in 2018
by Catarata as
Los Olvidados De Los Olvidados:
Un siglo y medio de anarquismo en España

© Carlos Taibo 2018
© Translation John Stewart 2023
© Illustrations, Jacobo Pérez-Enciso 2018

Permission for non-commercial use of parts of the text may be granted by the publisher on written request.
rights@merlinpress.co.uk

Printed in the UK by Imprint Digital, Exeter

The time will therefore come when the sun will shine only on free men who know no other master but their reason; when tyrants and slaves, priests and their stupid or hypocritical instruments will exist only in works of history and on the stage.
Condorcet

Contents

Preface to the English Edition	9
Preface to the Spanish Edition	11
What is Anarchism?	17
How Do We Explain the Strength of Anarchism in Spain?	23
Spain in the Second Half of the 19th Century	27
The First Steps of Spanish Anarchism	29
Catalonia, Andalusia …	34
Anarchist Terrorism	36
La Semana Trágica. Freethinkers, Republicans and Anticlericals	38
Ferrer i Guàrdia and the *Escuela Moderna*	40
The Emergence of the CNT	43
The Russian Revolution and *pistolerismo*	45
The Dictatorship of Primo de Rivera	49
The Second Republic	51
The Anarchists Were Not Republicans	55
The FAI	59
Trentistas and *Faístas*	63
The Internal Democracy of the CNT	65
Working-Class Neighbourhoods in Turmoil	70
An Alternative Society	73
Love of the Written Word	77
Anarchism and the National Question	80
The Revolution of 1934 in Asturias	83
The Elections of February 1936	86
The Military Coup of July 1936	88
A Revolutionary Dictatorship?	91

The Progress of the Civil War	94
Excesses and Violence	97
Mujeres Libres	99
The Agrarian Collectives	102
The Collectivisation of Industry	109
Beyond Self-management: Ecology and Growth	113
Anarchists in the Government	116
The Events of May 1937	121
Los Amigos de Durruti	123
The PCE and the End of the War	125
The Franco Regime	128
Exile and Resistance to Francoism	131
Reappearance After the Death of Franco	135
The Farce of Transition	137
The Libertarian Presence Today	142
The Relevance of Anarchist Thought and Practices Today	144
Chronology	147
Suggestions for further reading	150
Bibliography	151
Documentaries and other Films	156
Acronyms	157
Index	159

Preface to the English Edition

Some might wonder if there is any sense in publishing a history of the Spanish anarchist movement in the English language. I believe that three main arguments can be made for the value of this edition. The first is that the Spanish anarchist movement of the early 20th century was, without a doubt, the most powerful and influential anarchist movement on the planet and remains so even today. Secondly, the Spanish anarchism that emerged before 1939 provided a very suggestive terrain for social and revolutionary innovation and experimentation in an effort to construct a new world. Indeed, it has been suggested that Spain developed the strongest and most creative working-class culture of any that materialized in interwar Europe. Lastly, given our current situation, in which words like *ecofascism* and *collapse* are becoming current, it seems that libertarian ideas and practices are destined to resurface, in many cases in the praxis of peoples of the southern hemisphere, who, in their lived experience – as was the case for many Spanish anarchists a century ago – act in ways that reflect anarchist notions of, say, self-management and mutual aid.

In addition, I would like to identify two features of this work that seem to me of interest. I think of it as a little manual that affords a rapid and pedagogical approach to a complex subject. In this it is different from other texts, whether originals or translations, published in English. It seems to me that here the reader is not presented with a hagiographic work that effects an uncritical consideration of the Spanish anarchist movement. On the contrary, in these pages many of the movement's contradictions and shortcomings are highlighted, and, where appropriate, account is given of the sharp divergences of opinion on important issues that emerged within the movement.

Finally, this text would not have seen the light of day without the laborious and wonderfully voluntary effort of its translator, John Stewart. These pages are dedicated to him.

Preface to the Spanish Edition

My recent reading of popular books that seek to explain the Spanish Civil War to younger readers has left me feeling perplexed. In these books the role of the libertarian world is visibly diminished, to the point that it is difficult, if not impossible, to find any mention of, for example, the collectivizations that took place in 1936 and 1937 in the Aragonese countryside and in Catalan industry. Unsurprisingly, these works pay just as little attention to essential questions that, although marginal in revolutionary processes occurring elsewhere, had a singular strength and influence in Spain – issues related to self-management, decentralization, federalism, the question of nationality, and the role of the state and of the bureaucracy.

These works simply reproduce many of the commonplaces promoted by what some scholars have described as the *cultura de la transición* [culture of the transition, i.e. the political system after the death of Franco]. With respect to the pre-1939 libertarian world, the latter has juggled three distinct possibilities: it has encouraged oblivion; it has subsumed that world into the general magma of 'the republicans', displaying no need to introduce distinctions that are necessarily delicate; or the sharp scalpel of the expert is content with identifying in our anarchists a lamentable amalgam of violence, ignorance and primitivism.

Our libertarians have forever been made invisible. One knew they were there, but it was understood that their unhappy condition of grimy proletarians justified the noble decision to ignore them; or, which is the same, to make of them, as the Spanish-language title of this work has it, the forgotten among the forgotten. One should recall, however, that between 1868 and the end of the civil war in 1939, the Spanish labour movement was in its majority a libertarian movement. Anarchists played an unparalleled and decisive role in the struggle for the dignity and rights of the working classes. They led a genuine social revolution that deserves something more than the conspiracy of silence that has surrounded it in recent decades.

A few months ago, as this book took shape, I was asked (in a seemingly friendly tone) whether I was writing a laudatory pamphlet. I felt compelled to reply that I have nothing against pamphlets, which have often played a respectable role; and I immediately added that it is one thing to disclose one's sympathies for our libertarians, another to erase all critical considerations of what they were or did. Unlike the writings of most experts within the system, which rely on a vision of the world that is manifestly ideological – and therefore necessarily questionable – this text in no way attempts to conceal the sympathies I mentioned and assumes without duplicity that my sympathies are perfectly debatable.

One is constantly surprised by the gall of those 'experts' – professors, journalists, publicists – to whom I was referring. Immersed in their desire to demystify a subject that they themselves previously demonized, they fail to apply a similar criterion of demystification to the preconceptions that they themselves use. The result is easy to appreciate: much prudence and circumspection, much contextualization, when speaking of those they take to belong to their side; but when the topic turns to the libertarian world (and others), we are instead greeted by a rhetorical fusillade.

Many of these works evince the certainty that in 1936 and at several other historical moments, there was an established order – republican or Francoist – that was to be preserved against the excesses of the anarchists, without questioning where this order came from, nor to which interests it answered. In the best of cases, these experts tell us that, although naive and simple-minded, the anarchists were good people – they had their good aspects – until seduced by the temptation to put into practice their ideas ... All that is left is to identify, behind these discursive aberrations, a disturbing exercise in uncritical adherence to present-day attitudes that invites one to judge what happened eighty years ago based on the values and the presuppositions that are perhaps ours today. Again, with no discussion of what these values and perceptions actually signify, leaving them outside the lens of scientific rigour which many of our scholars claim to embrace.

Allow me to end this introduction with a few clarifications about what I wanted to accomplish with a text like this. I will emphasize, firstly, that unlike some of the works that have inspired it, this text is not strictly a book intended to be digested by 'young people', despite my not wanting to completely lose sight of that quality. I must also warn that the book is mostly focused on Spanish anarchism and touches only briefly on the overall context in which Spanish anarchism emerged: on Spain in the second half of the nineteenth century; on the political, economic, and social situation of the second republic; on the nature of Francoism; on the features of *la transición* – which invite the reader to contextualize the events.

In parallel, these lines of thought attempt to evaluate the different sensibilities, and their implications, within the Spanish libertarian movement, which was never a uniform whole, while at the same time resisting the temptation to which many authors have succumbed: that of reducing the history of this movement to its manifestations in Catalonia, with a few small incursions into Andalusia. It will soon become clear to the reader that, although the Spanish civil war lies at its core, this work is also visibly interested in what occurred before and after the war. It makes a merely instrumental and descriptive use of the term 'Spain', the most comfortable and fertile term to describe the geographic enclosure where the events it analyzes took place, but without any intent to assign it a meaning that might entail intolerable endorsements and identities. The book includes a bibliography – and a listing of documentaries and movies – incorporating a good number of texts, all in Peninsular languages [or, where possible, in English], that do not necessarily coincide with the perspective put forth in these pages.

Finally, I leave the reader with this modest book that comes out a century and a half after an Italian, Giuseppe Fanelli, visited Madrid and Barcelona to deliver the gospel of anarchism. In the certainty that among the inhabitants of *la piel de toro* [the land shaped like a bull's hide], many acts that can unproblematically be labelled as libertarian had already taken place. And in the certainty, too, that more and more [*otras y otros*, more women and men] will come.

What is Anarchism?

There are two different ways of understanding anarchism. The first views it as an ideology, or doctrine, that came to light between the late 1700s and the early 1800s, and that over time acquired a body of concepts developed by thinkers – mostly males – including Proudhon, Bakunin, Kropotkin and Malatesta. These concepts, which were rapidly embraced by workers and peasants, are principally those of self-management, democracy and direct action, federalism, and mutual aid.

The second way of understanding 'anarchism' – in this case the quotation marks are important – refers to a way of thinking and acting that, more-or-less consistent with the concepts just enunciated, has accompanied the human species from its earliest social condition. In this sense, it would be legitimate to attribute the status of 'anarchists', although the term 'libertarian' is preferable, to Chinese peasants from two millennia ago, to members of certain heresies in Medieval Europe, and to many of the native peoples today in America, Africa and Asia. While we commonly take the adjectives 'anarchist' and 'libertarian' to be synonymous (we shall consider them so in this work) the former term has a more ideological-doctrinal quality than the latter, which might well describe the daily conduct of people who, without ever having read Bakunin or Kropotkin, express through their behaviour their commitment to the principles of self-management, direct democracy and mutual aid. When in this work we give the adjective 'libertarian' this second, more specific meaning, we will try to expressly mention that decision.

What are the core ideas postulated by both the 'anarchist' and the 'libertarian' modulations just discussed? The first is that societies can and should organize in a non-coercive manner. Here one must emphasize what should be obvious: anarchists are not opposed to organization as such, despite what the former Minister of the Interior of Spain implied when, during a press conference, he declared that a 'surprisingly well organized' anarchist group was no longer operating ... The ideal of self-organization leads to that of self-management, i.e., the conviction that workers and human beings in general can and must collectively control all economic activity and all social relations, needing neither bosses nor managers, on the basis of federalism and decentralization. While the term 'self-management' became widespread during the French May of 1968, the concept was present much earlier, as is shown by the resolutions of successive congresses held from 1936 by the Spanish *Confederación Nacional del Trabajo* [CNT; National Confederation of Labour]. The essential question about the value and significance of work itself has found two enduring yet diametrically opposed responses in the libertarian world: the first values work as the nucleus and justification of human life and its progress, while the second insists that every imaginable effort must be made to reduce its burden and to suppress the numerous inconveniences that accompany it.

A second core idea is the concept of direct democracy. Rooted in a prior and active decentralization, it retains for us, the people, the maximum power of decision on all possible issues. We must reject all forms of delegation and representation, or accept them only according to very strict criteria that require delegates to merely support positions previously approved by us, within a framework of easy revocability of all delegation.

Thirdly, the notion of direct action empowers us with full control over what we do, without the mediation of external agencies that might interfere, correct, or orient our activity. Our means are then scrupulously adjusted to the ends we wish to achieve. Democracy and direct action entail a vivid rejection of all that is signified by leadership and personalism.

A fourth component of anarchism is the principle of federalism, an inescapable consequence of the first three precepts. The free federation theorized by Proudhon – especially his concept of confederation – is rooted in the autonomy of decision making in each component of the organization, within, again, a framework of general decentralization, and of course always on the basis of communal respect for agreements previously reached.

The fifth and last element is that of mutual aid. Theorized by Kropotkin among others, mutual aid situates the vigour of the principles of cooperation and solidarity at the centre of human societies, against the logic of competition and selfish individualism that is manifestly prevailing today. And it holds that there are numerous and substantial examples of animal societies that have prospered on the basis of these principles.

Taken together, these five tenets translate to support for an emancipatory process that, in the perception of the classical anarchists of the nineteenth century, was to encompass not only urban and factory wage earners – the proletariat to which Marx drew attention – but also broader layers of the population, surely including peasants, artisans, and other classless groups. Independently of whether or not this view has currency today, this emancipatory process necessarily entails a critique of many of the elements that articulate our contemporary reality, including capitalism, the State, patriarchal society, and the military.

The opposition to capitalism is present from the very birth of the libertarian movements of the nineteenth century. Those movements were committed to the rejection of salaried labour, of the commodity, of property and exploitation, of hierarchies and divisions. Property, in the eyes of the economist Flórez Estrada, was not only theft, as Proudhon had affirmed; it constituted, above all else, the root of all evils suffered by society. The principal explanation for the rise of libertarian syndicalism was none other than the desire to counter the excesses of capitalism – including, naturally, the colonial domination of yesterday and today, and all its crimes. Anarchist thinkers have, however, held contrasting opinions on science and technology, and the roles that these must play. While some have embraced their value enthusiastically for the progress of societies, others have been harshly critical of their contributions to the logic of capitalism, questioning the virtues of the presumed progress that has marked the course of our societies.

The rejection of capitalism was necessarily extended to that of the State, which libertarians understood as an apparatus in the service of capital, charged with developing repressive tools and mechanisms of domestication and control, such as the education system. Specifically, anarchists have always been highly critical of the political significance of elections, often describing them as farces that feed the optical illusions projected by representation and delegation. An article appearing in *La Idea Libre* of 1896 declared: 'We repeat: Voting is the same as annulling oneself. He who votes abandons himself to the will of others; he recognizes the right of unknown others to do as they will with the common interest. The ballot is the sign of political enslavement, just as the salary is the sign of economic slavery.' The inescapable fact is that a self-managed society built on direct democracy entails a full critique of the institution of the State.

Although it has its antecedents in the work of thinkers such as Bakunin, in the libertarian world the critique of patriarchal society was carried out above all by anarcho-feminism. It went well beyond the mere demand for equal rights for women and men and was rooted in the awareness of the endless power structures, material and symbolic, that force women into a permanent condition of disadvantage and submission to men. As will be seen later, during the Spanish civil war the *Mujeres Libres* [Free Women] movement was a fundamental milestone in the development of the of anarcho-feminism.

Finally, anarchism is by definition anti-militaristic, even if the critique of the military comes from quite distinct perspectives. The text on libertarian communism approved by the Spanish CNT on the occasion of the congress of Zaragoza in May 1936 identified a permanent army as a major threat, since 'under its influence, a dictatorship would be forged' that would end the revolution, and added that 'the armed people will be the greatest guarantee against any intent to restore the newly destroyed regime'. That same congress had openly rejected military service, in harmony with the marked antimilitarism that emerged in 1909 during *La Semana Trágica de Barcelona* [the tragic week of Barcelona], and with the resistance to militarization expressed during the civil war.

Behind all these ideas one can easily identify a profound defence of individual freedom – this was manifested, for example, in the agrarian collectivization in Aragon in 1936 – which has at least two important consequences. The first is that for revolutions to succeed, they must be the product of the freely-given popular support – a revolution against the will of the majority is not imaginable. The second is a clear awareness that we necessarily form part of the system we want to bring down, so that its logic, its principles, and its values exercise a powerful influence on our daily conduct. On the basis of these perceptions, the libertarian world developed an enormous capacity to predict the historical tendency of liberal pseudo-democracies, and of those peculiar forms of bureaucratic capitalism that were the Soviet systems.

Let us conclude by noting that various schools or currents are commonly distinguished within libertarian thought. One prevailing classification identifies four. The first is anarchist mutualism. Theorized above all by Proudhon and based on the idea that labour can be realized in both an individual and a collective manner, and that all profit and exploitation must be abolished, this perspective calls for the creation of mutual credit entities and the replacement of the State by a free federation of producers. The second and third currents, for which Bakunin and Kropotikin are the principal exponents, call for the revolutionary expropriation of capital and the abolition of private property, in favour of forms of collective labour. While the first adjusts remuneration to the output of each person, the second calls for the socialization of all goods, in such a way, to use Kropotkin's expression, that each person freely takes 'from the pile'. We must recall, to avoid any misunderstandings or clichés, that while many anarchist thinkers have declared themselves 'communists' or 'socialists', they have always added the adjective 'libertarian' to these labels. The fourth and last current, individualism, raises particular problems of characterization, since in the eyes of many libertarians it is situated far from anarchism itself. While many anarcho-individualists have indeed stood for the full autonomy of the individual – we have marked this as one of the foundations of libertarian thought – they have not all rejected the practice of collective work. It is therefore necessary to distinguish individualistic anarchism from the ultra-liberalism postulated by the American 'libertarians', immersed in an obscene defence of private property and individual interest, or what has often been described, mistakenly of course, as anarcho-liberalism or anarcho-capitalism.

It must be emphasized that the differences between these currents, especially between anarcho-collectivism and anarcho-communism, have not always been clear, and the corresponding terms vary in meaning by time and place. The irruption of concepts such as 'anarcho-syndicalism' adds further complexity if not confusion to these controversies. Suffice to recall that in Russia in the years after 1917, a sharp conflict arose between anarcho-communists and anarcho-syndicalists, while in Spain during the 1930s, anarcho-collectivists, anarcho-communists and, on occasion, anarcho-individualists shared a common organization of an anarcho-syndicalist character: the CNT.

How Do We Explain the Strength of Anarchism in Spain?

Much ink has been spilled on this decisive question. Before reviewing some of the answers that have been put forward, it is helpful to define the contours of the phenomenon from two distinct chronological perspectives.

The first of these perspectives, also the most prevalent, holds that the 'anomaly' – we will shortly account for this striking term – is only true from the end of the 1910s, when anarcho-syndicalism was established and gained strength, up to the end of the civil war in 1939. Before this, the course of events in Spain was not very different from other parts of Europe – that is, France, Italy, and Portugal – for example, the establishment of organizations sympathetic to Bakunin, acts of terror, and, ultimately, the rise of revolutionary syndicalism. In contrast, the second perspective emphasizes the fact that even today Spain retains the strongest presence of libertarian movements and initiatives of any country on the planet. The question then is whether this presence today is the product of an autochthonous and genuinely contemporary impulse, or if, on the contrary, it is mostly based on a phantasmagoric sequel to a glorious past.

Whichever perspective we assume, we must reflect on the term 'anomaly', which would describe the singular condition, establishment, and permanence of Spanish anarchism. This very striking term is employed consistently in both liberal and Marxist historiography. Here we will limit ourselves to asking about the virtues of the model of social development postulated by these two historiographies. This model has often led to countless aberrations in the form of colonial domination, the exploitation of slave labour, the marginalization of women in all social orders, fascisms, dictatorships, bureaucratic capitalism, and savage aggressions against the environment. Against this, is it not legitimate to consider a competing 'anomaly'?

What are some of the answers that have been given to the question heading this section? The first one – dismissible, frankly – merely claims that anarchism is a perfect adaptation to a presumed Spanish character, commonly described as anarchic, irrational, and, ultimately, religious. Of course, one cannot accept this description of the Spanish character, but supposing that such a thing does exist, there is still no reason to suppose that some feature of anarchism makes it a worldview adapted to such a character.

The second answer has doubtless enjoyed greater success, even though it hardly explains the success of anarchism in Spain. It recasts Spanish libertarians as the protagonists of a primitive and millenarian project that, in search of a happy Arcadia of the past, valorizes medieval notions of egalitarianism and expressly rejects modernity and progress. This interpretation, whose leading champion was perhaps the British historian Eric Hobsbawm, calls for at least two retorts. First, Spanish anarchists are not easily associated with an intent to reverse history. Rather, they very often, if incautiously, accepted the supposed benefits of science, and believed unquestionably in technological progress. Many of the Andalusian anarchists, who certainly seem to fit Hobsbawm's formula, often engaged in the dissemination of scientific and technical knowledge that liberals and socialists proudly disdained. It is true, however, that these attitudes towards progress were mingled with others that affirmed, almost always with good judgment, many elements of the communal tradition of the countryside, such as the protection of differences, forms of direct democracy, and the consistent practice of mutual aid.

Hobsbawm's thesis also warrants a response from another perspective: one which suggests, however cautiously, that what is contemptuously described as 'primitivism' and 'millenarianism' may well contain elements that are both healthy and worthy of our respect, and are critical of the supposed virtues of modernity and progress. These elements have been lucidly reclaimed by today's libertarian thought and by other currents and traditions. This aside, we must ask whether the endlessly retrograde elements that Marxist historiography – with Hobsbawn, in this case, at its head – identifies in Spanish anarchism are not also found in many movements that claim to be linked to Marx's work, including, certainly, Leninism itself. Whatever the case, we are obliged to conclude that the supposed 'anomalies' are actually not so anomalous.

A viewpoint to some degree similar to Hobsbawm's is that of the hispanist Gerald Brennan, who relates anarchism to the archaic character of the Spanish regime, incapable of adapting itself to modernity, steeped as it was in a permanent decadence. Hence the stagnation of that regime, the precariousness of mechanisms for people to participate in government, and the impossibility of carrying out substantial reforms. In Brennan's case it seems that anarchism – or at least rural anarchism, fundamentally Andalusian – was a moderately logical response to the character of the regime, though once again Brennan interprets the response as religious and millenarist, rooted more in faith than in reason. According to one version of the events, the very common distinction between a primitive anarchism and one less so was used by the Catalan bourgeoisie to attribute many of the real or imagined excesses of the libertarian world in Catalonia to the influx of people from other areas of Spain.

The idea that anarchism was a functional response to the regime ruling Spain has been expressed many times. Among the relevant features of the regime were a visible social polarization, the near non-existence of an emerging middle class, and the manifest ineffectiveness of the State that – hyper-centralized, bureaucratized, militarized, and repressive – was incapable of addressing the needs of the populace. The State was nothing other than an apparatus at the service of the ruling classes.

Conditions were unequivocally favourable to the deployment of forms of direct action, and justified the widespread rejection of a centralizing, bureaucratic, and cold socialism, implanted in the institutions. To this was added, above all in Catalonia, the libertarian world's remarkable capacity for adaptation in conflicts over matters of nationhood, often accompanied by the defence of differentiated local cultures, desirous of maintaining their independence.

The libertarians of Spain gave rise to a mostly undogmatic movement that, lacking an established and shared body of theory, easily adapted itself to disparate settings and moments. Efficient in terms of communication, having a simple and direct style, very distant from that of politics of the day, this movement often assumed different forms in different parts of the country, in urban and rural environments, in work centres and in neighbourhoods. As a result, it revealed a stronger link to immediate reality than the theorizing of Bakunin or Kropotkin. Beginning in the 1910s, it equipped itself with a mass organization, the CNT, that brought together quite disparate initiatives and sensibilities. Thus, in Catalonia, the most industrialized part of the country, a visible relationship was established between anarchism on the one hand, and the intelligentsia and scientific and technological progress on the other. By way of contrast, in Andalusia and Aragon one easily perceives the nexus between anarchism and the agrarian collectivism described by Joaquín Costa, as manifested by the existence of communal assets for the use of landless peasants, within, again, forms of direct democracy and mutual aid.

Spain in the Second Half of the 19th Century

The Spain of the second half of the 19th century was a county burdened by enormous problems and inequalities. To take just one data point, life expectancy was very low – perhaps 33 years, at certain times, in working-class Barcelona – due to malnutrition and the impact of epidemics. In 1877, in a country in which the Catholic Church and its defence of the traditional family was firmly established, 72% of the population was illiterate. Many Spaniards sought the path of emigration, almost always to America. The phenomenon was especially strong in Galicia, but it was also present in Catalonia, in Asturias, and in what today is called Castile and León. The main destinations were Argentina, Cuba, and Brazil.

The economy had a fundamentally agrarian character. The workforce employed in crop and livestock farming was almost five times greater than that in industry. Modernization efforts had been held back by the congenital weakness of the bourgeoisie and its inability to gain power. Rather than allowing a significant part of church wealth to end up in the hands of the dispossessed, the confiscation of ecclesiastical property created an agricultural proletariat made up of more than two million landless peasants, who were subjected to a crude exploitation. The *Guardia Civil*, created in 1844, was tasked with controlling and harshly repressing whatever protests occurred.

Despite a boom in the textile industry and its exports at the end of the century, and the fact that foreign investment in mining increased, that the railway system was expanded, and that the populations of cities like Madrid and Barcelona grew significantly, an entrepreneurial bourgeoisie was still lacking. The weight of industry was concentrated in Catalonia and the Basque Country – also, for a time, in some areas of Andalusia – while banking developed in Madrid and in Catalonia, and later more successfully in the Basque Country, aided by the mining and steel industries.

After the failure of the first republic in 1873-1874, a genuine political farce was installed, under a decrepit monarchy, staged by two large political parties that were both complicit in a system that remained despotic, centralized, and militarized. The introduction of universal male suffrage in 1880 by no means ended the despotism and electoral fraud perpetrated by liberals and conservatives. The hyper-centralization of the system triggered the eruption of what were initially regionalist movements, but later developed into Catalan, Galician, and Basque nationalism. To death throes of the past – like the third Carlist war, fought between 1872 and 1876 – were added military coups and the very high maintenance costs of the armed forces. Completing the panorama were the enormous resources spent on the important bureaucratic apparatus in the colonies. The end of the colonial adventure in Cuba, Puerto Rico, and the Philippines led to a simplistic reflection on the conditions of Spain itself, such as that carried out by members of the so-called *generación del 98* [Generation of 1898].

The First Steps of Spanish Anarchism

If we take the adjective 'anarchist' in the first of the senses previously considered, it can be said that anarchist ideas first arrived in Spain in 1868. It is true, however, that earlier initiatives had paved the way. There had been the influence exercised by some of the first socialists, interestingly labelled 'utopian socialists', such as that of Cabet and Saint-Simon in Catalonia, and that of Fourier in Andalusia and Madrid. These thinkers and their followers engaged in essential debates regarding the role of the individual in emancipatory transformation, well portrayed by Fourier's repeated assertions that the degree of emancipation of a society is measured by the degree of liberation of its women.

In the 1820s there were instances of luddite practices, directed at destroying the machinery of the industrial revolution. The first resistance-oriented workers' societies emerged from this early magma, in conjunction with insurrections by landless peasants. While the first workplace organizations or trade unions worthy of the term appeared, according to one version of the facts, in 1840, it was not until 1855 that the first attempt to call a general strike was made, in defence of the right of association, and against strenuous working hours. The incipient labour movement was the object of overt persecution, though in parallel there were early attempts, usually short-lived, to establish what today we would describe as co-operatives. But perhaps the most noticeable influence on what would soon be the first stirrings of Spanish anarchism was exerted by Proudhonian federalism and mutual aid, disseminated above all by Pi i Margall.

A. Fanelli

In 1868 an Italian, Giuseppe Fanelli, arrived in Spain as an envoy of the International Workingmen's Association (IWA), which at that time was marked by the conflict between two opposing perspectives. The first, reflected in the figure of Marx, supported the seizure of State power and urged the formation of a vanguard that was to guide the proletariat – the social class that was to drive the revolutionary process. The second viewpoint, linked to the person of Bakunin, argued that people are capable of governing themselves, rejected the notion that the institution of the State could play a revolutionary role – thus demanding its dissolution – and suggested that, along with the proletariat, the task of emancipation required the participation of peasants, artisans, and members of the most overlooked sectors of the population. In the eyes of Bakunin, the State generates a fiction of freedom and democracy that blocks the liberating drives of the people. The corresponding aberrations were all the greater in the case of the 'State socialism' promoted by Marx, which Bakunin perceived as the worst tyranny imaginable, a power that would brazenly serve an arrogant and despotic elite of experts and scientists.

To a significant extent as a result of Fanelli's mission, in 1870 the *Federación Regional Española* [FRE, Spanish Regional Federation] was formed, affiliated with the IWA and mostly based in Catalonia and Andalusia. The echoes of the Paris Commune in 1871 led to a severe repression of the FRE and its members. An FRE manifesto from the same year vividly describes one of the dimensions of the social conflict at that time:

> They call us lazy because we ask for a reduction in working hours, as recommended by hygiene, science, and human dignity – they, who do not have nor have ever had calluses on their hands, who perhaps have not produced a useful idea; eternal parasites that are the cause, by their unproductivity and monopoly over capital, of the misery that corrodes the bowels of society.

The following year, 1872, saw the definitive split within the International between those we will call 'authoritarians' – the followers of Marx – and 'anti-authoritarians' – the supporters of Bakunin. The latter maintained the International until 1877, dispensing with the General Council and Marx. Many anti-authoritarians defended collectivism, looked forward to the suppression of the State and social classes, and rejected parliamentarism. This agenda was embraced by many Spanish internationalists. Most of the incipient local labour movement took the side of the anti-authoritarian faction, initiating a process that stretched all the way through the civil war waged between 1936 and 1939.

There was some participation by Spanish anti-authoritarians in the insurrections that occurred in 1873 – perhaps the most notable was that of Alcoy (Alicante), during the first republic. They generally believed that the republic had no interest in altering the rules of the game. After the FRE was outlawed, at the start of 1874, it spent seven years in hiding, to reappear in 1881, above all among the peasants of Andalusia and within the newly constituted *Federación de Trabajadores de la Región Española* [FTRE; Federation of Workers of the Spanish Region]. Meanwhile, worker and peasant organizations that later would be called 'unions' began to materialize, and conflict between anarcho-collectivists and anarcho-communists was making itself felt. Among the latter, 'affinity groups' were frequently formed, only to disappear very quickly, in response to the incipient bureaucratic tendencies of the traditional organizations. Perhaps the two most prominent figures of the events of those years were Anselmo Lorenzo and Fermín Salvochea.

One more fact completes the panorama of a period marked by repression and the libertarians' disdain for official politics, which they found distasteful. This was the rivalry between the anti-authoritarians and the nascent *Partido Socialista Obrero Español* [PSOE; Spanish Socialist Workers' Party], which, created in 1879, was explicitly reformist, moderate, and open to the rules of the game set by the system. The *Unión General de Trabajadores*

[UGT; General Union of Workers], a trade union network linked to the Socialist Party, was founded in 1888; it settled with ease in Madrid, the Basque Country, Asturias, and Castile. The Socialist Party aspired to seize political power and promote the nationalization of significant sectors of the economy.

Catalonia, Andalusia ...

The incipient libertarian movement was stronger in Catalonia – which had a large and combative working class – and in Andalusia – by virtue of a fundamentally spontaneous process – than in Madrid, a city that was more administrative and less working class. This initial geographic configuration persisted over time; the movement was fundamentally urban in Catalonia and of a mostly rural nature in Andalusia, though Catalan anarchist organizations welcomed many immigrants from rural parts of the country, who as a result were added to the ranks of local workers.

From the start and until 1939, however, libertarian organizations were also present in other areas of Spain. They were strong in Valencia and Murcia, in Aragon, in La Rioja, on the west coast of Galicia, in significant areas of Extremadura and La Mancha, and in the two archipelagos [the Balearic islands and the Canaries]. In addition, there were important cells in Madrid, Asturias, and in the Basque Country.

The condition of early Andalusian anarchism, which was perhaps more in line with the second modality of anarchism already discussed, the one whose base character is spontaneous rather than ideological-doctrinal, was based on a crude analysis of the untenable social and political situation in the countryside. In its initial form, Andalusian anarchism might seem to conform to the image of the 'primitive rebels' so dear to the British historian Eric Hobsbawm, an unequivocally negative image contrasting with the supposed modernity and rigour of Marxist movements. Yet these supposed or actual primitive rebels were much less susceptible to the thrall induced in so many emancipatory movements, often with tragic consequences, by parliamentary games or the myths of growth and technology. Andalusian anarchists frequently engaged in practices of direct action such as robbery and looting, the burning and occupation of land, and the exercise of acute pressure on strike-breakers. They often espoused the redistribution of land over its collectivization. Even so, many Andalusian anarchists – particularly in the provinces of Malaga, Sevilela, and Cáadiz, and in specific moments also in that of Cordoba – were not so distant from the ideals and actions of industrial workers in Catalonia, and among them were plenty of educated peasants who read books, articles, and pamphlets out loud to their illiterate comrades.

Finally, Andalusia was frequently the scene of bloody events ending in violent repression. Incidents in Jerez involving *Mano Negra* [Black Hand] in 1882, were with all probability the result of a manipulation by the authorities. Although the FTRE distanced itself from the clashes, many of its members suffered the violence unleashed by the government. Again, in Jerez, ten years later, in the context of an insurrection launched with hardly any preparation – which was common in those times – hundreds of day-workers occupied the city with the cry of 'long-live the social revolution and death to the bourgeoisie'. What followed, once again, was an extremely harsh repression.

Anarchist Terrorism

The last decade of the nineteenth century and the first of the twentieth saw the extension of a phenomenon that was often described as anarchist terrorism. It took the form of attacks against government officials, such as the assassinations of Cánovas de Castillo in 1897, and, later, those of Canalejas (1912) and Dato (1921), though the latter likely perished at the hands of paid assassins. There were also various failed attempts to assassinate Kings Alfonso XII and Alfonso XIII.

The most notorious attempt against the king was carried out by Mateo Morral in Madrid in 1906. Other attacks targeted the bourgeoisie and the nobility – such as the attack at the *Liceo de Barcelona*, in 1893 – or against the Church – the bombs thrown on the occasion of the Procession of the Corpus Christi, also in Barcelona, in 1906. Behind many of these events were infiltrations and provocations by the police, resulting in very severe acts of repression that time and again decimated the libertarian movement, – which, despite everything, recovered quickly.

These attacks were usually actions by individuals operating outside of established organizations. Even though social conditions were appalling, a reality that certainly suggested violent responses, most members of the dispersed libertarian movement were not involved in the violence, and indeed some criticized it bitterly or fought to construct an expressly pacifist discourse. Tolstoyan pacifism, which in many of its dimensions had a libertarian character, was a growing phenomenon. For this reason, the intentionally distorting image of anarchism given at the time, which in many ways has reached us today, cannot be accepted. And yet, the exhibition organized in Zaragoza in 2010 to commemorate – this may not be the best term – the hundredth anniversary of the founding of the CNT, opened with the reconstruction of one of those attacks. Should the visitor have had the good sense to ignore it, gunshots rang out periodically in all the rooms.

A concept that was frequently employed in the anarchist world during those years was that of the 'propaganda of the deed'. Despite the distortions it suffered, the concept had a general character, well beyond that of terrorist violence. Rather, it referred to an endless number of possible behaviours, such as forms of civil disobedience, strikes, and, more broadly, attitudes that question the prevailing morality.

La Semana Trágica. Freethinkers, Republicans and Anticlericals

Between 25 July and 2 August 1909 a series of violent clashes that came to be known as the *Semana Trágica* [Tragic Week] took place in Barcelona. More an improvised mutiny than a genuine revolution, it was a spontaneous anti-militarist revolt against the levy of soldiers to be sent to Africa. Three years earlier, the Algeciras conference had established the bases of what would become the Spanish protectorate in Morocco. Many buildings were burned, churches in particular, and, as was customary, the mutiny provoked a very severe repression. Several thousand people were detained, and some executed, the most notorious victim being Francesc Ferrer i Guàrdia, the founder of the *Escuela Moderna* [Modern School], an initiative to which we will soon turn.

The libertarian thought of the period, rather syncretic and undogmatic, maintained a lively rapport with other currents of thought, such as those represented by freethinkers, republicans, and anticlericals. Many enlightened anarchists were freethinkers and masons, and many libertarians shared with republicans their admiration for the French Revolution. Anarchism and republicanism had a fluid if tense relationship, with points of both agreement and disagreement. Anarchism was by definition more oriented towards the working classes, while republicanism was linked more closely to the middle classes and the petty bourgeoisie. Though separated by irreconcilable differences regarding participation in State institutions, some anarchists provided electoral support for republicans in specific situations.

While today the role of anticlericalism is much reduced in libertarian circles – there are active currents advocating a suggestive dialogue between anarchists, Christians, Jews, and Muslims – most libertarians of the past were furiously anticlerical, in great measure as a reaction to the belligerent collaboration of the Catholic Church with government institutions and with the most traditionalist interests. That said, the report on libertarian communism approved by the CNT congress held in May 1936 stated that 'religion, a purely subjective manifestation of the human being, will be recognized as long as it remains relegated to the sanctuary of individual conscience, but in no case may it be considered as a form of public ostentation or of moral or intellectual coercion'.

Ferrer i Guàrdia
and the *Escuela Moderna*

In Spain the first steps towards a new and emancipatory pedagogy were taken in the mid-nineteenth century by the socialist followers of Fourier and Cabet. This new pedagogy was a constant preoccupation for the nascent labour movement. 'There is no workers' congress that does not raise the problem of education,' wrote Díaz del Moral in his *Historia de las agitaciones campesinas andaluzas* [History of Andalusian peasant unrest].

Around the turn of the twentieth century, Francesc Ferrer i Guàrdia emerged as a key figure in this area. He endeavoured, through the project of the *Escuela Moderna* [Modern School], to promote knowledge and behaviours that would bring an end to tyranny and exploitation, and would do so without privileges, hierarchies, and rewards and punishments. When Ferrer was asked where the idea of creating a new school had come from, he replied, 'Well, simply from the school of my childhood, because I wanted to do the total opposite of what it was'. Ferrer i Guàrdia's model was anti-militarist, anti-clerical, and, in many ways, anti-patriotic.

The *Escuela Moderna* also had its critics. Some found it abhorrently doctrinaire, and not always unambiguously libertarian since it incorporated the perspectives of freethinkers and republicans. Also, as was the case for much of the labour movement of the 19th century, both in Spain and abroad, the school often expressed a naive worship of science and reason.

In the three decades following its founding, the ideas of the *Escuela Moderna* were carried on by the so-called rationalist

schools, which were particularly active during the second republic – there were around one hundred in Catalonia at that time. The *Consejo de la Escuela Nueva Unificada* [CENU; Council of the New Unified School], founded in Catalonia during the civil war, promoted a free and public education based on rationalist principles. Rationalist schools were created in many other parts of Spain as well.

Today, debates about education are frequent in the libertarian world. There are essentially three viewpoints. The first calls for the socialization and self-management of public education, the second for the creation of free or libertarian schools far removed from the conventional system of education, while the third calls into question the very concept of education itself, since, from this perspective, formal education will always mask a will to coercion and domestication.

The Emergence of the CNT

Revolutionary syndicalism had its origins in France, where its doctrine was codified in the so-called Charter of Amiens of 1906. These ideas soon arrived in Spain, where, for better or worse, and not without controversy, they were associated with what would eventually be called 'anarcho-syndicalism', i.e. an attempt to transpose the anarchist perspective to the context of workplace organization.

There are persistent disagreements about when anarcho-syndicalism first made its appearance: while the year 1923 is often invoked, some instead refer back to the period of *Solidaridad Obrera* (Workers' Solidarity), a syndicalist network created in Catalonia in 1907. Three years later, in 1910, in the wake of *Solidaridad Obrera*, the *Confederación Nacional del Trabajo* (CNT; National Confederation of Labour) was founded, first as a Catalan organization, and then, the following year, as a Spanish entity. Although soon outlawed – it had to wait until 1917 to be legalized – the CNT experienced a gradual growth of its ranks: just over 25,000 in 1911, 50,000 in 1916 and perhaps 75,000 in 1918.

Let us summarize in a few points the programme of the CNT. The first was the principle that the union must become the basis of all production, distribution, and the organization of the society of the future, which it had the obligation to prefigure. In this sense the union was tasked with combining short-term objectives – improving working conditions – and longer-term goals – the emancipation of workers. Another important feature was the adoption of the general strike as a prelude to social revolution, in conjunction with various types of direct action, such as strikes themselves, the occupation of work sites, boycotts, and sabotages. A third golden rule was federalism, which guaranteed a remarkable autonomy for member unions, and enabled decision-making to flow from the bottom up. 'If no one works or lives for you, let no one decide for you,' went a well-known saying.

Although the First World War was very beneficial to many employers in Spain, the benefits, as usual, hardly ever reached the workers. The resulting labour conflict induced a first rapprochement between the CNT and the socialist UGT. This was made concrete in 1917 in the course of important general strikes, in which socialists played a greater role than libertarians. In 1919 in Barcelona the CNT emerged triumphant from a major labour conflict, that of the *Canadiense*, which, after extensive labour support for the strike, resulted in the recognition of the eight-hour working day. A radical paralysis of public services was achieved during the strike, and so-called 'red censorship' was exercised on the newspapers of the Catalan capital.

At the end of the 1910s territorial forms of organization began to appear within the CNT, to the detriment of industry-centric modes of organization. This process benefited the more libertarian sectors and weakened those that had a more trade focused character. The strengthening of the libertarian current was underpinned by the intransigence of employers, who refused to concede to labour demands, and by the influence of the Russian revolution, at a time when membership had grown significantly. According to one estimate, in 1919 the CNT had 715,000 members.

The Russian Revolution and *pistolerismo*

Although the First World War led to a remarkable growth of industrial production in Spain, the prices of many goods rose faster than wages. Added to the resulting problems was the impact of the revolutionary process that took place in Russia in 1917, encompassing the February revolution, which in effect overthrew the Tsar, and the October revolution, which brought the Bolsheviks to power.

The Russian revolution was met with lively interest – and, initially, open admiration – in the Spanish libertarian world. Perhaps the best example is the CNT's request in 1919 for provisional membership in the so-called 'Third International', promoted by the nascent Bolshevik regime. However, the visit to Russia by a representative of the confederation, Ángel Pestaña, ended with the publication of very negative judgments about the system that was taking shape. There followed a rapid distancing between the two organizations, and in 1922 the CNT committed itself to support a revived International Workers' Association, or *Asociación Internacional de Trabajadores* [IWA-AIT]. The *Partido Comunista de España* [PCE; Communist Party of Spain] was born in those years, in the wake of events in the emerging Soviet Union. The relationship between the CNT and the PCE was always difficult, reaching its greatest strain during the civil war.

Many of the differences separating Spanish and Russian anarchism from Bolshevism reflected those of fifty years earlier between Bakunin and Marx in the days of the First International.

Salvador Seguí (1886-1923)

In the libertarian perception, the Bolsheviks had progressively annihilated the autonomy of grassroot elements; had proscribed all competing movements; had established a hierarchical and pyramidal regime in which the party and the State overlapped; had proceeded to militarize the economy, within a framework of State capitalism far removed from any practice of self-management; had proclaimed themselves the representatives of the workers; had laid the foundations of a bureaucracy separated from the population; had created conventional armed forces; and, finally, had equipped themselves with various largely unregulated repressive agencies. The resulting system, with its hierarchy and with its distance from the people, greatly recalled the rules of capitalism that the Bolsheviks believed they had defeated.

The last years of the 1910s and the first years of the 1920s were also indelibly marked by a rather negative phenomenon: what would come to be called *pistolerismo*. Employers, who had created the 'free unions' financed the activity of gunmen who acted with the open consent of the authorities. The latter were determined to enforce a law that permitted the police to shoot those who fled from them – or were said to want to do so.

Certainly, there were anarchists who simply sought to benefit from robberies and murder. And while at the end of the nineteenth century most of the libertarians responsible for attacks acted individually, in the 1920s they often received organic support from the CNT, determined to respond to the bosses' terror. The onus of organization fell onto affinity groups, small organizations of people brought together by common sympathies and projects. That formula, which at times yielded a vanguard dedicated to raising the political consciousness of the ignorant populace, made infiltration by the police significantly more difficult.

Of the more than a thousand people who lost their lives between 1917 and 1922 due to *pistolerismo*, three quarters were workers. Among those assassinated was the most prominent figure of the CNT at the time, Salvador Seguí, and Francesc

Layret, a lawyer who represented many syndicalist federations. Seguí had argued for direct action that instead of engaging in attacks and assassinations was carried out by workers themselves in the workplace, having the strike as its principal tool. This type of action had yielded important results, as attested by the already mentioned strike at the *Canadiense* in 1919.

The Dictatorship of Primo de Rivera

In the last years of the 1910s and the first of the 1920s the Spanish government faced several military crises and very delicate social circumstances, and its political system was increasingly discredited. As a result, between 1923 and 1930 Spain was ruled by a dictatorship headed by General Primo de Rivera, whose position benefited visibly from the military landing at Alhucemas in Morocco, which served to obscure the disaster of Annual in 1921. It is certainly true that compared to the Franco regime after the civil war, the dictatorship of Primo de Rivera appears rather bland.

Although the CNT was initially tolerated, it was eventually declared illegal, along with many associated organizations, such as libertarian schools. The dictatorship instead clearly benefited the UGT which, in collaboration with employers and with the regime's encouragement, participated in the deployment of corporatist formulae. Also present was a trade unionism tied to socially-oriented catholicism, wholly non-confrontational and incapable of competing with the programmes of the CNT and UGT. While Primo de Rivera put an end to *pistolerismo*, the arrests and prosecution of libertarians continued, and basic legal guarantees were non-existent.

Not without paradox, the dictatorship of Primo de Rivera led to the establishment of the *Federación Anarquista Ibérica* [FAI; Iberian Anarchist Federation] (we will turn to this later) and to violent responses by anarchist groups such as the so-called *Los Solidarios* (The Comrades). This group brought together figures such as Buenaventura Durruti, Franciesco Ascaso, and Juan García Oliver, and was frequently involved in robberies, described as 'expropriations'. The CNT also participated actively in various plots aimed at bringing down the regime, such as those recorded in 1926 and 1929. Within the union a leadership made up of syndicalist veterans was gradually replaced by much younger leaders, mostly linked to affinity groups. Underlying this shift was the long-standing tension between supporters of a less political syndicalism, often described as 'apolitical', and those inclined towards a decidedly anarchist syndicalism. The CNT returned to legality in 1930, during General Berenguer's interregnum, and in the following year the second republic was declared.

Buenaventura Durruti

The Second Republic

The second Spanish republic was born in an international moment indelibly marked by the negative effects of the crisis of 1929. It did so in a country that had experienced important changes in the previous decades. Among these was the significant growth of cities, above all Madrid and Barcelona, due to processes of internal migration. During the 1910s and 1920s the incidence of epidemic-related mortality decreased significantly, accompanied by improvements in health and nutrition. In the shadow of a monarchy in open decline, and with the delicate heritage of the Moroccan war in the background, smallholders remained clearly dominant in the north of the country, while large estates prevailed in the south, where rural unemployment – at times reaching two-thirds of the workers – was the daily reality.

In December 1930 a failed uprising took place in Jaca, in Huesca, which, led by Captains Galán and García Hernández, who were executed, briefly proclaimed a republic. The actual advent of the latter resulted from municipal elections held a few months later, in April of 1931. Republican-socialist candidates prevailed in a majority of provincial capitals even though they received fewer votes overall than candidates who supported the monarchy. One should note, however, that in the rural areas, the mainstay of the conservative vote, freedom to vote one's conscience was conspicuous by its absence. King Alfonso XIII left the country soon after.

The history of the five years separating the proclamation of the republic from the military coup of 1936 can be split into

three phases. The first, marked by the figure of Manuel Azaña between April 1931 and the end of 1933, has commonly been termed the *bienio reformista* [reformist biennium]. The power of the traditionally parasitic classes was supposedly replaced by that of an enterprising bourgeoisie, though not without hitches, such as the coup d'état attempt by Sanjurjo in 1932, and not without frequent complaints about the incapacity of the republican-socialist authorities to pursue credible policies such as agrarian reform. The second phase, the so-called *bienio negro* [black biennium], followed the elections held in November 1933, won by the right-wing *Confederación Española de Derechas Autónomas* [CEDA; Spanish Confederation of Autonomous Right-wing groups] of José María Gil Robles and the centrist *Partido Radical* [Radical Party], led by Alejandro Lerroux. In 1934 a revolt erupted in Asturias, harshly repressed, to protest the de facto incorporation of the CEDA into the government. In February 1936, finally, the Popular Front, which united various leftist political forces, won the new elections, albeit by a narrow margin. The resulting government had little time to develop a programme, which in any case could not be called radical.

There has been much debate about the role played by the CNT in the elections of 1931, 1933, and 1936. Although it is a controversial issue, the common view is that the *cenetistas* [members of the CNT] were not particularly committed to abstention in 1931 and 1936 — in the latter year many of them were in prison — and that, on the other hand, they abstained en masse in 1933. It is true that the defeat of the left in that year has frequently also been attributed to the then recent recognition of the voting rights of women, most of whom would have supported conservative candidates.

The republic was, in any case, a State whose economic and social makeup was very weak, incapable as it was, for example, of collecting the taxes necessary to undertake the reforms that were postulated on paper. The republican years proved to be ones of permanent crisis, as manifested by extensive unemployment, often very prolonged, and by visibly intransigent employers who were determined to preserve their privileges. In such conditions, the disenchantment of many workers is hardly surprising. Despite the statutes of autonomy approved for Catalonia, the Basque Country, and Galicia (there was no time for the last to come into force), the demands for decentralization that came from those three regions were never fully satisfied.

The Anarchists Were Not Republicans

It is often assumed that, especially during the civil war, Spanish anarchists were republicans. Nothing could be further from the truth. The relationship of the libertarian world with republican institutions was usually tense, and despite possible points of agreement, profound divisions persisted. This was so, first of all, because of the obvious fact that anarchism is ontologically opposed to all forms of government, and the republic is evidently one such form. For the majority of Spanish libertarians, what emerged in April 1931 was an anodyne bourgeois republic that achieved little more than the introduction of sharp new instruments for the marginalization and exploitation of workers and peasants, welcoming into the ruling elite many defectors from the preceding monarchy. The idea that the republic aspired to modernize Spain, and to convert it into a country similar to the 'western democracies', evaded any serious debate over the meaning of the term 'modernization' and of the realities of these supposed democracies.

While the advent of the republic aroused little enthusiasm in the libertarian world, many saw it as an opportunity that, thanks to greater freedom, permitted certain possibilities of action that were previously closed off. This did not stop, however – and here we return to the main thesis – the proliferation of disagreements between Spanish libertarians and the regime after 1931. These disagreements were reflected in local insurrections, harshly repressed by the republican government, which were promoted by some of the most radical sectors of the libertarian

world, and in decisions such as that in favour of abstention in the general election of November 1933.

The overwhelming majority of anarchists and anarcho-syndicalists understood that the republic had failed in every one of its supposedly most successful projects. It was manifestly incapable of pushing forward an agrarian reform, which at any rate aspired to little more than fixing the many problems affecting Spanish capitalism. During the black biennium the republic even encouraged a genuine counter-reform. The privileged classes preserved the bulk of their power unscathed, despite the burden of a permanent economic crisis and very high levels of unemployment and poverty. Even the left wing of the Socialist Party, headed by Largo Caballero, insisted that the *Azañista* republic was determined to block many reform initiatives. Not only that: the facts are that the republic preserved a good part of the centralizing logic of the State, and this despite what the appearance of Catalan, Basque, and Galician autonomies might suggest. It cannot be denied, however, that through an appreciable effort in education, the republic brought about a significant reduction in illiteracy.

Things were no better in the area of labour. The *jurados mixtos* ['mixed juries' to mediate in disputes between employers and workers] promoted by the PSOE in 1931 were clearly beneficial to the UGT. Made up of employers and workers, and often with the participation of the government and a weighty bureaucracy, they explicitly set out to reduce the importance of the CNT and to limit the right to strike and other modalities of direct action that typically lead to negotiations between workers and employers without intermediaries. There is no doubt that such Republican apparatuses triggered radical responses, weakening the position of the more moderate *cenetista* syndicalists.

For good measure, the *Ley de Defensa de la República* [Law for the Defence of the Republic], evidently designed to facilitate the repression of anarcho-syndicalism, allowed the authorities to suspend legal guarantees, a reminder of many legal norms in force during the monarchy. During the reformist biennium other questionable laws were passed, such as those for 'public order' and 'vagrants and criminals'. Repression was not limited to the black biennium, as evidenced by the events in Casas Viejas, in Cadiz in January of 1933, when 22 people were executed by the *Guardia Civil*, and many other episodes. The effects of the creation of the *guardia de asalto* [assault guard] were present everywhere. It was a force created by the republic itself and charged with carrying out the repression of protests in cities. In a scenario in which arrests of *cenetistas* were frequent, it is hardly surprising that the latter viewed conditions during the black biennium as no different than before, when Azaña and the leftist republicans were in power. To all the above was added the certainty that the republic reacted timidly and complacently towards members of the military who were preparing a coup. In the words of Chris Ealham, the republic was founded on a middle-class fantasy expressed as the recurring demand for a world of order. If today the republic seems more attractive because of the inevitable comparison with Francoism, a cold consideration of its reality compels us to maintain an openly critical distance that is regrettably lacking in many who situate themselves on the political left.

The FAI

Established in Valencia in 1927, the *Federación Anarquista Ibérica* [Iberian Anarchist Federation; FAI] had its origins in libertarian affinity groups. It first emerged among militant anarchists who believed that the CNT was weak and was sliding into a reformist syndicalism – what was sometimes called *'trentismo'* [thirtyism], a political faction which we will turn to shortly – increasingly removed from the programme of revolutionary transformation. There was an attempt, then, to inject clearly anarchist content back into the life and positions of the CNT.

According to one estimate, the *Federación Anarquista Ibérica* – which also harboured a small number of Portuguese libertarians – had 5,500 militants in 1933, 3,500 in 1936 after successive waves of repression, and 160,000 during the civil war. During the first years of the republic, the FAI, now transformed into an assault force against employers and the police apparatus, was the main protagonist of what was called 'revolutionary gymnastics'. Under its banner, and with leading figures such as Durruti, the Ascaso brothers, and García Oliver in their midst, insurrections erupted in Andalusia, Aragón, Catalonia, Extremadura, León, La Rioja, and Valencia. These insurrections often involved raising the red and black flag over town halls, declaring universal fraternity and libertarian communism, abolishing money, and burning the property registry. Though generally disjointed and ill-prepared, and unable to outline a fully-fledged revolutionary programme, the revolts were undeniably useful learning experiences for what was to come, i.e., the military coup of July of 1936.

The FAI underwent important changes from 1933 onwards, after the arrival of personalities who were more loosely connected to street fighting. Doubtless the most significant was Diego Abad de Santillán. The liberation of prisoners became a fundamental task for the federation, which in 1936, despite appearances, was on the same path of integration into governing institutions as pursued by the CNT.

In Catalonia, where it had its greatest presence, the ranks of the FAI were swelled by recent immigrants from areas such as Murcia and Alméria, at a time when the ranks of the *trentistas* consisted mostly of Catalan workers, descendants of immigrants who had already settled in Catalonia. This despite the fact that some of the more emblematic figures of the FAI were Catalan – such as Federica Montseny or the already-mentioned García Oliver – or were schooled in the social struggles in Catalonia. The terrible economic situation of the second republic led many of those most affected, usually unskilled workers who had recently arrived in Catalonia, to join the ranks of the FAI. There was undoubtedly a certain generational dimension underlying the confrontation between *faístas* and *trentistas*, at least in Catalonia if not in the rest of Spain. The former were usually younger and had been forged in the fighting during the days of *pistolerismo*, when they had had to face the harassment suffered by the CNT, in an environment marked by a pronounced lack of freedom. The latter belonged to an older generation and expressed a calmer and more reflective sort of syndicalism.

There has been much debate on the nature of the FAI: was it a vanguard that behaved in a more-or-less authoritarian manner, or, on the contrary, was it a horizontal and assembly-based organization like the CNT, at least on paper? This question has received two answers. The first affirms, with no room for doubt, that the FAI established a vanguard aimed at controlling the CNT, thus upending many anarchist postulates, and that its behaviour was authoritarian and hyper-controlling. The second instead views the FAI as a pressure group whose purpose was to safeguard revolutionary ideas that were seen as threatened.

The task, in this perspective, was to prevent the CNT from being taken over by external forces that would reduce it to a union like the UGT, which unproblematically adapted to the laws and interests imposed by capital and the State. Whichever view is correct, it should be remembered that the FAI was not a secret organization – in specific circumstances it had, of course, an undeniably clandestine character – so it seems very unlikely that it could develop strategies as intricate as claimed by either of these interpretations.

Trentistas and *Faístas*

During the second republic, between 1931 and 1936, the libertarian world was afflicted by major divisions. The most significant conflict was felt within the CNT itself – it had some 800,000 members in late 1931 – that pitted a group known as the *trentistas* against the *faístas*. Although the boundaries between their respective positions were not always clear – surely not all anarchists were in the FAI, nor did all *trentistas* shy away from the anarchist label – the broad terms of the disagreements between the two groups were as follows.

By *Trentismo* one understands a doctrinal position that received its name from the so-called *manifiesto de los treinta* [manifesto of the thirty], signed in August 1931 by a handful of prominent CNT activists, including Juan López, Joan Peiró and Ángel Pestaña. In time the *trentistas* formed the *sindicatos de oposición* [syndicates of the opposition], excluded from the Confederation in March 1933 and reintegrated in May 1936 at the Congress of Zaragoza. In its essence, *trentismo* stood for a syndicalism that sought alliances outside the libertarian world, above all with the UGT. In some of its manifestations it also approached the republican parties and Catalan nationalists, and on occasion it became involved in conventional political struggle, as shown by its flirtations with the prospect of participating in municipal elections in Catalonia, or, in the case of Pestaña, the creation of the *Partido Sindicalista* [Syndicalist Party]. In any event, the *trentistas* stood for a more gradualist syndicalist activism to build the strength of the CNT as, in their opinion, conditions for a revolutionary insurrection were not present. In parallel, *trentistas* were proponents of large, compact, and well-run federations that were organized by industry rather than by territory. This principle fitted uneasily with libertarian projects of decentralization and location-specific interventions in working-class neighbourhoods.

We have already pointed out some essential features of the militancy that formed the FAI. Breaking with the reformism embraced by many *trentistas*, the militants who joined the FAI were determined to use violence in defence of an insurrection that was expected to occur in the very near future. Thus, if in the eyes of the *trentistas*, the radicals, by means of their disruptive actions, made it impossible for the republic to progress in desirable ways, to the *faístas* it became evident that their moderate rivals saw in the republic qualities that did not exist.

There were at least two other conflicts plaguing the libertarian world in this period. The first, subterranean but omnipresent, thus less overt than the great debates regarding organization and action, opposed people impregnated with hedonism, who sought the pleasures of life, to proponents of an ethic of work, who embraced a harsh puritanism, rejecting gambling, alcohol, and tobacco. This second position was certainly dominant in libertarian cinema and theatre. The other collision, which to some extent overlapped with that of *trentistas* and *faístas*, was between militants who wanted to build a parallel society gradually, over time – an alternate society that would also serve as an education in revolution – versus supporters of an immediate insurrection that would end capitalism and give birth to a new society overnight.

The Internal Democracy of the CNT

During the 1930s the CNT was an assembly-based organization – on paper, at least – in that it practiced direct democracy, and, forgoing leaders and managers, operated according to the principle of federalism. Although the materialization of this ideal was occasionally problematic, on the whole the Confederation's machinery of democracy was far more solid and credible than those of parties such as the *Izquierda Republicana* [Republican Left], the PSOE or the PCE, or of unions such as the UGT, all organizations in which personalities and hierarchical processes were the order of the day.

Within the base of the confederal world, discourse was far more open and plural than in other organizations, and a very original and admirable model emerged, at the cost, in practice, of enormous personal and economic sacrifice. In those years the CNT had officially only a single full-time employee, the secretary of the confederal committee, even though, according to one version of the facts, the work of other individuals, in particular those involved in the confederal press, could well have required thirty salaried positions. It would have been difficult to identify the 'leader' or 'leaders' of the CNT, something that was not true of the Republican Left – the party of Manuel Azaña, the PSOE, where the names of Indalecio Prieto or Francisco Largo Caballero would immediately stand out, and for the PCE, those of José Díaz or Dolores Ibárruri.

The rank and file of the CNT had a very positive view of the union, in contrast to the sentiments aroused by the typical political party. This image, which owed much to a determined struggle for better working conditions, explains why in delicate moments CNT militants closed ranks around the Confederation. The CNT's actions were visible in everyday life and, as is the case today for many organizations of the political left, it had no need of intermediaries to make it function. It did so very efficiently, despite its means of communication being far more precarious than those of today. It seems beyond dispute that in explaining why so many workers joined the CNT, the most significant fact was less the workers' proximity to anarchist or anarcho-syndicalist ideas, and more just the certainty that the Confederation would fight for their interests. Perhaps there was also the certainty that the CNT was unlikely to 'sell out' its members, removed as it was from leadership games and politicking.

Naturally this singular reality was not free of problems. These were rooted in the tension between two clearly defined groups: the militants at the base, and a diffused 'cupola' made up of those who were called 'influential militants'. Among the former, the organizational principle of the Confederation, based on assemblies, direct democracy, and federalism, was found to be reasonably satisfactory. Although the organization tried to adopt decisions unanimously, on occasion the majority principle was applied. To repeat, the operations of the unions were tightly constrained by their ultra-democratic rules.

Nevertheless, over time there emerged a cupola with unique characteristics. Personalism and leadership appeared largely accomodated within the cupola, and there was no evident competition for positions. To be part of this cupola it was not necessary to hold or have held jobs of significant responsibility. The effect was a structure that was internally horizontal rather than pyramidal, circumstance that perhaps explains why it was very difficult to identify the leaders of the CNT, often leading outsiders to the conclusion that such leaders did not, in fact, exist. Logically, in clandestine situations the role of this cupola was strengthened.

Seldom was criticism directed towards these 'influential militants'. Rather it seems they aroused admiration for their knowledge, their courage, or their suffering in prison. Their status derived from their merits and their dedication, conditions that, according to one view of the facts, blurred the sense of the term 'leader'. At a rally held in December 1932 Durruti claimed that 'those whom the bourgeoisie calls "leaders" are workers whom everyone knows, and their way of life is identical to that of any unfortunate worker. They stand out because they have the courage to choose the worst position in the fight, to be on the front lines, stop a bullet and fill the prisons.' It was understood, moreover, that these so-called leaders fully represented the interests of those below them. Relationships of friendship and acquaintance were decisive, and there were neither formal procedures for accessing the cupola nor for designating committees responsible for selecting members.

A major and delicate effect of the above was that the great questions – the debate between *trentistas* and *faístas*, or, even more so, the discussion in 1936 about a possible participation in the republican government – were not shaped by the opinion of the militant base, and it was no easy task to alter the views embraced by the 'influential militants'. Added to this – and perhaps it could not have been otherwise – there were frequent misalignments and disagreements deriving from the autonomy of the unions and the application of the federalist principle. Conversely, the programmatic discussions that took place during the congresses ran along more open and participatory lines, allowing the great strategic questions to benefit from a different channel of discussion.

During the civil war the nexus between the militants at the base and the 'influential militants' changed, as many of the latter shifted their work to organizations inserted into State institutions, further removing them from the confederal world. In parallel a certain cult of personality emerged, the greatest example being the figure of Durruti, particularly after his death. There was also a proliferation of supposed militant leaders who –

all men and often very *macho* – did not disdain rising through the ranks of the republican army. The solidly established leadership that emerged proceeded to make decisions for others, entering into agreements with traditional political forces and bending to the logic of State apparatuses. The revolution, meanwhile, was led by anonymous men and women who gave meaning to the collectivizing experience in the fields and the factories. In essence, these developments were the result of contrasting operational principles of workplace organization: management exercised from above versus a creative imagination rooted in self-management from below.

It is important to emphasize the characteristics of the people who joined the CNT and, in general, the libertarian world. The overwhelming majority of its members were self-taught workers. The Soviet writer Ilia Ehrenburg hit the mark when he referred to the Spanish anarchists of the 1930s in the following terms: 'The anarchism of the Spanish trade unionists is not the anarchism of the literary types of the cafés, who confuse Bakunin with Stirner [the main anarcho-individualist thinker], anarchism with erotism, liberty with libertinism. The Spanish anarchists go to work. Their leaders do not drink, nor do they frequent the red-light district; Spanish anarchism is a sort of religious order of severe observance.' This human material was certainly different from that which won in the Russia of 1917, under the leadership of another cupola, that of the Bolshevik party, made up above all by petty-bourgeois intellectuals. Very few people in the Spanish libertarian world were of anything other than humble origin. Perhaps because of this, and with certain exceptions like Fermín Salvochea, Ricardo Mella, Diego Abad de Santillán, Isaac Puente and the members of the Urales family – Federica Montseny's family – it produced few intellectuals and thinkers.

One final observation. According to Ángel Pestaña, only a third of the militants of the CNT were anarchists. We should ask ourselves how many of the remaining two thirds were anarchists without knowing it, conforming to the second version of the category we sketched out at the beginning of this work. Could it be that, in a supremely paradoxical way, the 'influential militants' of 1936 actually lagged behind those ordinary peasants who, though formally not anarchists, were nevertheless organic to a spontaneously libertarian tradition?

Working-class Neighbourhoods in Turmoil

The CNT was more than just a workplace organization. It was often active in neighbourhood committees, which, according to one activist's description, acted as the eyes and ears of the Confederation. These committees made their presence felt in all areas, fostering a very rich social life, providing education, and initiating campaigns of the most diverse sorts. Local federations often allowed the union to insert itself into everyday life, by means of a movement in which politics, union activism, culture, friendships, and family relationships were all brought together into an inextricable mix, rooted in solid personal relationships. Neighbourhood committees were of decisive importance, moreover, in moments when the CNT was repressed and banned.

The urban situation administered by the committees – the case of Barcelona, suggestively studied by Chris Ealham, is surely the clearest – often consisted of impenetrable neighbourhoods into which the police forces seldom dared to venture. Given a manifest suspicion of bourgeois legality – a suspicion that fed alternative forms of financing, including bank robberies – there was a general conviction that workers were morally superior to the owners, a superiority that enabled urban workers to forge a 'we' in solidarity. Not only that: there was also a proud resistance to bourgeois culture, to which one of proletarian character was opposed.

Many forms of protest grew from these foundations, drawing on the principles of direct action. It is often said that the libertarian movement was overly invested in a future revolution, thus ignoring more immediate issues. This is evidently not true. It is enough to recall initiatives such as the collective search for employment for the unemployed – the CNT made overt efforts to integrate the unemployed into its ranks – or, not without intimidation, the decision to eat without paying in restaurants, or the practice of collectively confiscating goods from shops whose abuses and irregularities were denounced. But we must also mention the creation of tenant unions that stood up to the frequent usury of landlords. *Escraches* [bullying actions] and other interventions were executed with the aim of relocating residents who had been expelled from their homes. The rent strike in Barcelona in 1932 led to the refusal by many tenants to leave their homes, and during the civil war the urban working class proceeded to occupy numerous homes that had been abandoned by their owners.

Key elements of the libertarian presence in working-class neighbourhoods were the athenaeums, cultural centres that disseminated ideas, trained militants, engaged in cultural diffusion (theatres, movies, etc.), created consumer cooperatives, cared for the elderly, and organized excursions and sports. While some were manifestly independent, others were linked to the FAI or to the *Juventudes Libertarias* [Libertarian Youth]. They welcomed people of all sorts, not only militants from the anarchist world, though men were in the clear majority, as with the neighbourhood committees. Frequent objects of repression and closure, operating under conditions of precariousness and lacking resources, the athenaeums were nevertheless able to maintain their activity even when syndicates or movements identifying as anarchist were forced underground.

Before the civil war the athenaeums were mainly focused on culture. They housed rationalist schools, developed courses and conferences, set up libraries – often the backbone of the athenaeum – created theatre groups and orchestras, and disseminated knowledge related to everyday life in areas such as health, sexuality, and science. When war broke out they also became involved in the supply of food, the creation of defence committees, and security. They then set aside the cultural dimension in favour of other purposes, more ambitious and mobilizing, which in some cases became the construction of libertarian communism. Unfortunately, as the months went by, the athenaeums were forced to devote much of their energy to defending themselves from harassment by republican institutions.

An Alternative Society

The libertarian world promoted ways of living at odds with those imposed by the Spanish society of the time. Let us summarize them by considering the notions of naturism, neo-Malthusianism, free love, and proposals for a new urbanism.

Naturism grew out of earlier efforts to protect nature, and, in more political and social contexts, from the demand for the abolition of private ownership of land and water. Among its manifestations we find nudism, vegetarianism – and in general the search for a healthy and frugal diet – the practice of hiking and of the contemplation of the landscape, and the defence of Darwinism against religious visions of creation. It also involved a wide variety of sports activities (gymnastics, swimming, athletics, cycling, boxing), and criticism of professional sports. 'True sports must be practiced freely, without prizes or payments,' we read in a publication of the FAI. Inevitably, the use of sports for the sole benefit of the bourgeoisie and of dictatorial governments was also contested; sports were to be granted a social dimension born from below.

The defence of neo-Malthusian postulates was common. It often surfaced as the highly questionable imperative to 'improve the race', possibly even limiting the number of births. On occasion, however, neo-Malthusianism drew on Kropotkin's notion of mutual aid and thus emphasized the values of collaboration and solidarity against the logic of competition.

As for free love, it was a central element in a set of initiatives that included the affirmation of free relationships, detached from churches or courts; the stimulus given to sex education, far from religious prejudices and bourgeois hypocrisy; the demand for improvements in hygiene and prevention of disease; the distribution of birth control methods; and, more broadly, the creation of a new social matrix in which the freedom of women would be realized. A decisive role in the diffusion of these ideas was played by the magazine *Estudios* and by doctor Félix Martí Ibáñez.

On the topic of sexuality there were many contradictions, such as the frequent condemnation of masturbation, or at least suspicion of it. Or the many reservations aroused by homosexuality, often the object of a pitying respect that assumed there is a normal and a deviant sexuality. Horacio M. Prieto, an important *cenetista*, even affirmed that 'unnatural pleasure will be sanctioned as degrading and will find just repression in the psychological reaction of the people …' How curious this suggestion of regimentation, disqualification, and punishment, from one sector of the CNT, so incompatible with the much more widespread affirmation of free and open relationships.

We have spoken of the desire to encourage a new urbanism, based on cooperation and mutuality, and aimed at dissolving the distinction between urban and rural areas. This sometimes took the form of proposals for what was called 'city-country', and for cities with no more than one hundred thousand inhabitants, even if this entailed the demolition of existing buildings. The author Alfonso Martínez Rizo, in a little book of 1932 entitled *La urbanística del porvenir* [*The urban planning of the future*] affirmed that, for hygienic reasons, in places like Madrid or Barcelona 'it would be necessary to demolish more than 80% of the houses'. The uneconomic, unhygienic, and antisocial dimension of large cities was frequently emphasized, along with the rejection of the 'bourgeois business' of real estate speculation and usury supported by the authorities. In addition to advocating a general tenant strike, the expropriation of certain sites and the construction of homes by unions was encouraged.

Proposals for the transformation of daily life and of human communication, carefully studied by Dolors Marin, did not end there. Let us recall, for example, the importance that groups dedicated to the study of Esperanto had in the libertarian world. Or the frequent rejection of alcohol, perceived as a poison employed by the bourgeoisie to keep workers apart from the revolutionary struggle. Moderation was affirmed, and criticism was levelled at cafes, bars, and cabarets, to which unions, athenaeums, libraries, and rationalist schools were opposed. Many anarchists were fervently anti-clerical, a reaction to the obscurantist and reactionary role played by the Catholic Church in Spanish society at the time. The desire to symbolically escape the control exercised by political institutions and the Church was expressed by giving children novel first names – *Acracia, Floreal, Germinal, Helios, Libertaria, Luz* – and the adoption of a libertarian calendar that celebrated the anniversary of the Paris Commune and May First.

Love of the Written Word

The libertarian world has always had an overt fascination for the written word. That fascination has survived to this day, as is shown by the proliferation of publishing houses and periodicals. These publications find suggestive spaces for promotion in the anarchist book fairs held yearly in several dozen localities, where, in addition, debates are organized on a wide variety of subjects.

According to one estimate, between 1869 and 1939 some 900 periodicals (magazines and newspapers) and more than 3,000 books and pamphlets were published. Throughout those seven decades, the predominant reader was the self-taught worker, and there was no shortage of workers and peasants who, though illiterate, listened with rapture to readings of articles published in the anarchist press, or to excerpts from the works of Bakunin and Kropotkin – often leading to sudden illumination in their minds.

'The crusaders of the cause are usually great readers of newspapers, pamphlets and propaganda books (sociology, as they say), and even elementary works of history, geography and the physical and natural sciences,' writes Díaz del Moral in his history of Andalusian peasant unrest. And indeed there was a bit of everything in the texts published by our libertarians. There were, of course, the classics of anarchist thought. The great writers of yesterday were also present, including Cervantes, Quevedo, Valera, Clarín, and the French naturalists. In all publications there was room for poetry that often sang the problems of the poor, the struggles of the workers, of free love, and of human progress. Certainly, the popular novel and the serial had their places, and although they frequently portrayed a type of free and insubordinate woman, they usually depicted heroes who were inevitably male, altruistic, and supportive, at war with selfish people. Moreover, an irrepressible desire for scientific dissemination was evident, almost always accompanied by texts of a practical character.

However much names like Ricardo Mella or Federico Urales might resonate for us today, Spanish anarchism was fundamentally a movement of workers and peasants, and thus did not produce great thinkers. It nevertheless promoted high-quality publications, such as *La Revista Blanca* [The White Review], where tensions between the intellectual sectors of anarchism and the workers' movement were frequently discussed. Prominent writers such as Unamuno, Azorín, Camba, Baroja, and De Maeztu transitioned ephemerally through libertarian publications, often displaying a sort of aestheticizing anarchism. Soon, however, a process of mutual distancing took over: writers such as those mentioned quickly moved away from the libertarian world, and within the latter there appeared visible misgivings regarding intellectuals and the avant-garde. That said, a few writers in their maturity displayed some affinity for libertarian or liberalizing ideas – for example, Ramón Sender and León Felipe – and there is the literary landscape of Catalonia, where the rapport between workers and intellectuals was more fluid. It is nevertheless striking that the great writers associated with the republic – think of Antonio Machado or Federico García Lorca – had barely any ties to the libertarian world, in which, to repeat our verbal formula, the forgotten among the forgotten came together.

Principally supported by athenaeums and schools – and now we are far from the written word – among libertarians there was a clear commitment to cinema and what was called 'social theatre'. Of a supposedly realist nature, not always compatible with an improving and puritanical morality, many of the scripts of the time inevitably seem naive to us today. Music underwent a remarkable parallel development, represented by a handful of anarchist songbooks and frequently influenced by French cabaret music and by songs originally written by Argentinian and Mexican anarchists. During the civil war, in which hymns such as *Hijos del pueblo* or *A las barricadas* became famous, there was a tremendous outpouring of songs related to the war itself and the revolution, almost always sung by the many workers' choirs.

Anarchism and the National Question

The relationship between anarchism and the national question, both in general terms and in the Spanish context, is another topic that has raised much controversy. In the libertarian world the topic of nations and nationalisms gave rise to two opposed viewpoints. The first was perhaps best represented in many of Bakunin's texts, which reflected an active participation in the struggle for the liberation of the 'oppressed peoples', and asserted without reservation what today we call the right to self-determination. The second viewpoint is seen in these words, enunciated by the *Consejo Federal de la Región Española* (Federal Council of the Spanish Region) in 1871: 'We are enemies of the homeland! Yes, we want to replace the petty feeling for the homeland with the immense love for humanity, the narrow and artificial [national] borders for the great homeland of work, for the world.'

It is nevertheless possible to bridge these two perspectives. An example of this is the anti-centralist vocation of Spanish anarchism, expressed as the notion of federalism. Élisée Reclus, the French anarchist geographer, found that in Spain the federal principle was clearly well-established, thanks to the country's natural division into areas that had conserved a remarkable degree of geographical particularity. The natural setting of the Iberian peninsula has given rise to distinct historical regions, inevitably leading to the active defence of those spaces, whether communal or municipal. So-called 'libertarian municipalism' played a leading role in this defence. Thus, it seems that the anarchist world is by definition 'independentist', and consequently upholds the independence and sovereignty of all political units, as long as they remain unbound to the State.

In the same vein, there was an overt interaction between the CNT and what we will term, in an unequivocally diffuse manner, 'Catalanism'. Much of the Catalan libertarian world inserted itself into a local tradition characterized by the presence and action of very horizontal and self-managing social movements. It was less insurrectional and more gradualist than in other parts of the Iberian peninsula. In this context, federalism, and thus the defence of Catalan identity, operated to some degree as a response to the doctrinal impossibility of championing a Catalan State, while the rejection of the State institution in local anarchism often overlapped with the rejection of the Spanish State in Catalan nationalism. Out of this magma there emerged an active collaboration with Catalanism in order to overthrow the dictatorship of Primo de Rivera, a lively relationship between veteran syndicalists, usually *trentistas*, and Catalan republican politicians, and ties between the intelligentsia and anarchism that were significantly stronger than in other places. A few words from Salvador Seguí summarize, perhaps, the underlying theme of many disputes: 'The Catalanism of those who lead the *Liga Regionalista* [Regionalist League, an organization of bourgeois Catalinists] is false. These people put their class interests, that is, the interests of capitalism, above any other interest or ideology [...] Whereas we, the workers, would lose nothing with an independent Catalonia. Quite the contrary, we would gain a lot. The independence of our land does not scare us.'

That said, among immigrant workers, or at least recent immigrants, there was a rejection of the language and culture of Catalonia, especially during the second republic. Even today the identity narrative of Spanish nationalism is not infrequently accepted in the libertarian world, almost as if it had a placid and neutral character. It is as if the institution of the State is certainly to be questioned in its political, economic, and social dimensions, but not in its construction of a nationalist imaginary and identity. That the acronym CNT refers to a *National* labour confederation is significant, raising issues that are not always confronted fully and convincingly.

Nevertheless, many anarchists, freed from the cult of the idea of Spain, or simply oblivious to its meaning, defended the right of 'any region' to separate from Spain. During the civil war it was suggested that if Catalonia were separated militarily from the rest of the Spanish territory, a declaration of independence could follow. There were frequent proposals aimed at creating a Catalan CNT that would escape the control of the Spanish CNT. Another response to these problems took the form of rather pointless attempts to create pan-Iberian organizations. This happened in the FAI and in the *Mujeres Libres* [Free Women] movement, which saw the participation of individuals from Portugal.

Importantly, the libertarian world actively rejected the colonial policies enacted by the Spanish rulers in Cuba and the Philippines, and advocated for negotiated solutions, or, where appropriate, for independence itself, while also refusing to join the ranks of the military. Unfortunately, Spanish anarchists had little influence in Spanish-occupied Morocco, despite the many suggestions made to that effect – a serious error given what happened in July 1936. Although not organized by libertarian organizations, the failed Popular Olympiad in Barcelona that same year was more than just a response to the Summer Olympics in Berlin. The event was intended to lead to the general rejection of all competition between States and nations, which was to be replaced by competition between representatives of cities, open to athletes from non-independent states, and with the notable presence of women and both professional and amateur athletes.

The Revolution of 1934 in Asturias

In October 1934 the incorporation of the CEDA into the republican government, perceived as a sort of fascist coup – leaders of that political organization had announced their desire to emulate the models of Hitler's Germany and Mussolini's Italy – provoked a revolt, or revolution, in Asturias. The socialist world played a greater role in these events than the anarcho-syndicalist one. It was surprising that the socialists resorted to force, contrary to decades of their practice. In the event, the revolt initiated a process that brought together socialists, anarchists, and communists, as reflected by the slogan *Unios, hermanos proletarios* [UHP; Unite, proletarian brothers]. This rapprochement exposed in the Asturian CNT a difference in attitude – paradoxically, perhaps, similar to that of the *trentistas* – compared to the other federations of the trade union.

The *Alianza Orbera* [Workers' Alliance] that followed was weighed down by false steps. Although agreements between the cupolas of the unions were established, it proved difficult to effectively unite workers in the factories and mines. The workers, now armed, eventually found themselves compelled to self-organize, without, and often against, union leadership. The Socialist Party failed to push forward the revolutionary process. What happened bore a certain similarity to the events that took place soon after in Catalonia, in July 1936: again, many workers took destiny in their own hands, turning their backs on union leaders who were instead determined to endorse institutions that workers saw as at the root of many of their problems.

Libertarian communism was proclaimed in some localities, and private property and money were abolished, so that one could speak of the 'Asturian commune'. There was undeniably much improvisation in this, and no real plan or programme for the revolution.

The Asturian revolt was followed by an extremely violent repression directed by General Franco. The reaction was facilitated by the fact that the revolution found little support in other areas of the country, enabling the government to concentrate its forces in Asturias. Only in Catalonia and the Basque Country were there sympathetic movements of any relevance. In the former there was a nationalist revolt in which the CNT did not participate. When a Catalan republic was proclaimed, this revolt ended with the arrest of its president, Companys. In the Basque country violent clashes occurred in Mondragón and Eibar. Outside of Asturias the CNT barely mobilized, primarily due to the exhaustion produced by the 'revolutionary gymnastics' of the previous years. The repressive consequences were serious in all of Spain, leading to numerous arrests, the closing of union premises, and the application of a severe censorship.

The Elections of February 1936

The Popular Front, running against an alliance of the CEDA and moderate republicans, received a similar number of votes in the elections of February 1936 as its opponent, but the former enjoyed a comfortable majority in terms of seats. While the CNT did not join with the Popular Front, which was composed of socialists, republicans, various communist groupings, and nationalists, it also did not campaign in favour of abstention, thus ensuring the triumph of the Front. Underlying this posture was the desire to obtain the release of its prisoners, some ten thousand, jailed as a consequence of the insurrections of the previous years and the Asturian revolution of 1934.

With Azaña once again in a prominent role, the government of the Popular Front – which restored Catalan institutions – adopted policies that proved to be overly moderate and timid, producing obvious disappointment. As evidence of this is the rejection of proposals emanating from various sectors of the Socialist Party demanding the nationalization of certain economic sectors, and the absence of credible measures to confront the danger of a military coup. The very high numbers of the unemployed and the fact that agrarian reform was simply ignored by the large landowners, without further consequences, convinced the militants of the CNT that the new government was unwilling to alter old repressive policies and to open new horizons of social justice. Actual power, in other words, remained in the same hands as always.

The months from February to July were highly turbulent, with numerous attacks and street incidents involving people of widely disparate ideologies, though marked by the increasing prominence of the militants of the *Falange Española* [the Spanish Phalanx, i.e. Spanish fascists]. The assassinations of the monarchist leader José Calvo Sotelo and of the republican lieutenant José de Castillo had an enormous symbolic weight. And there was no shortage of violent clashes, unpublicized, that were reminiscent of events a few years before in Casas Viejas. Among these was an incident in Yeste, in Albacete, where a score of peasants who were defending their land were assassinated by the *Guardia Civil* in May 1936.

The CNT, for its part, was actively preparing to confront a military coup that seemed very close. In May, in Zaragoza, it celebrated a congress which saw the rapprochement of *faistas* and *trentistas*, in good measure the product of the repression suffered by all as a result of the revolution of October 1934 in Asturias. A major consequence of the congress was the readmission of the opposition unions, essentially *trentitas*, that had previously been expelled.

The Military Coup of July 1936

On the eighteenth of July 1936 a military coup took place. Clearly in the service of the wealthy classes and the church, and soon associated with the name of General Franco, its main nucleus was in Africa. The coup was responded to with lamentable complacency by the republican leaders, who were reluctant to hand over weapons to the labour unions and were often preoccupied with sterile negotiations with the rebels. This resulted in the unjustifiable loss of cities such as A Coruña, Granada, Sevilela, Vigo, and Zaragoza. Admittedly, the degree of organization of the CNT in these cities was not comparable to what the confederation exhibited, most notably, in Barcelona.

One must recognize the outsized role played by the libertarian world, or at least its most committed sectors, in responding to the military coup. That response also had, of course, the support of military and police personnel close to the republic and of many militants from left-wing parties and the UGT. The libertarians were decisive in Catalonia, in Valencia, and in a good part of Aragón, and important in Madrid, in Asturias, in the Basque Country, and in many areas of Andalusia. Despite the refusal of the majority of republican leaders to give weapons to the unions, workers sought armaments on their own, as for example in Barcelona, where ships anchored in the harbour were taken by assault. Many ordinary workers had learned to distrust republican leaders, so it was all the more surprising that the leadership of the Confederation immediately formed a courteous, if not cordial, relationship with the republican authorities. The workers' distrust was rooted in the suspicion that many political leaders

preferred what they imagined Franco would represent over the forseeable consequences of putting weapons into the workers' hands.

In Barcelona – the city where Francisco Ascaso was murdered in the dockyards, along with many comrades – the defence committees of the CNT-FAI played a very important role (in those months the two organizations presented themselves as a unified whole). These committees had matured during the days of *pistolerismo* and in the insurrections under the republic and the revolution in Asturias. Initially dedicated to self-defence, the committees were clandestine organizations of the CNT that soon began preparations for a general insurrection or a response to a military coup. They functioned as a somewhat *sui generis* type of affinity group. Following the coup of July 1936 the defence committees established neighbourhood revolutionary committees, which took on tasks such as the supply of food, the maintenance of refectories and hospitals, street surveillance, and the creation of operational units of militants. At their side were workers' militias, formed by volunteers, that challenged many of the rules typical of tranditional armies. According to a relatively extensive assessment of the facts, the libertarian militias were adept at guerrilla warfare but less skilled when it came to conventional warfare.

What began in July 1936, during what Hans Magnus Enzensberger called the 'short summer of anarchism', was a 'social war' that overlapped with a 'civil war'. Both wars saw the emergence of a resistance against fascism unlike anything seen in Germany, Italy, or France. The ensuing conflict was therefore not merely a confrontation between liberal democracy and fascism. As Murray Bookchin has emphasized, the conflict was also not simply a prelude to the Second World War. Spain was an exception, because its attempt to confront the problems of its modernization led to a movement that advocated and enacted a social revolution – with all its imperfections – instead of a mere adaptation to the socio-economic environment, or merely the attempt to apply of ideas formulated in one or other intellectual or political laboratory.

A Revolutionary Dictatorship?

The scenario that emerged in the days immediately following 18 July 1936 came as a surprise to the CNT. The confederation had certainly shown itself capable of responding to the rebels, but the effects of its lack of a strategic programme were evident.

In Catalonia the leadership of the confederation opted to collaborate with the other 'anti-fascist' forces. Hence the birth of the *Comité Central de Milicias* [Central Committee of Militias] which, far from reflecting workers' power, exemplified a model of collaboration between classes. The government sought to isolate the burgeoning workers' committees, justifying its conduct by invoking the imperative to collaborate with other political forces to defeat the fascists. And, somewhat surprisingly, it was suggested that if this were not done, a 'revolutionary totalitarianism' would prevail. Although at first there was a weak attempt to create a defence committee with an overwhelming majority of the CNT and the UGT – each of these unions counted on the order of a million members in July 1936 – at the Confederate level the possibility of an alliance with the socialist union was never seriously considered. Subsequent events would have taken a different turn had the CNT not collaborated with and, soon after, integrated into republican institutions. This aside, one must ask what sort of revolutionary totalitarianism or dictatorship could have otherwise emerged. To suppose that the anarchists would have acted as the Bolsheviks did in Russia twenty years earlier showed a dramatic lack of faith in their ideas and practices, all the more so since the libertarian view held that it is governments themselves that by their inherent logic give rise to dictatorships.

Instead, in weakening the revolutionary force, the confederate leadership paradoxically strengthened a counter-revolutionary project that, opposing all class-specific politics, legitimized the State and political parties, asserting the political principle of 'national unity'.

The major consequence for the CNT was a dramatic loss in credibility and influence, which masked an enormous ingenuousness and a poor ability to move in unfamiliar terrain. Moreover, the decision by the confederal leadership to split from the greater part of its core beliefs was adopted by the 'influential militants' without prior consultation of the militancy, i.e. the cadres of the CNT and FAI.

The outcome of all the above was that false disjunctions were imposed – 'social revolution or democracy', 'anarchist dictatorship or democratic government' – and two distinct processes unfolded: while the cupola of the CNT decided to renounce libertarian communism – however provisionally – many of the militants of the base enthusiastically gave themselves over to its construction. If the intention of the leadership was to defend the social revolution against attempts by various political institutions to control or indeed cancel it, the facts are that collaborations with those same institutions blocked any consistent effort in that direction.

For many textbook Marxists these facts are explained by affirming that in Spain, where a full 'bourgeois revolution' had yet to take place, the 'objective conditions' that permitted a 'socialist revolution' were not present. Certainly, in the eyes of many of these scholars the 'objective conditions' exist only when convenient, after formidable exercises of manipulation of the historical data, as in the Russia of 1917. These people simply dismiss out of hand all facts that are incompatible with their worldview. The complexity of the historical situation, and of its analysis, is shown by the fact that Spain in 1936 was no longer a semi-feudal country. The importance of the peasantry in its economy had receded in previous decades, and the industrial proletariat was expanding, circumstances that created a more complex scenario than that envisaged by vulgar Marxist interpretations.

The Progress of the Civil War

It would be a gross error to assume that the civil war was a military cakewalk for the rebel army. Although the rebels were able to gradually conquer territory without serious setbacks, it took no less than 32 months to defeat a rival markedly depleted in its capabilities, despite having a clearly more professional force and being better supplied. The units that opposed the Francoist army were built almost from scratch, were equipped with limited weaponry, and faced serious food supply problems. In the last phase of the war the republican army was compelled to mobilize 17-year-old males.

The coup of July 1936 received the strong backing of big business, large landowners, and the Church, all determined to preserve their manifest privileges. It also had the support of parties like *Falange Española*, and benefited from the discontent of many military personnel. The Francoist side consolidated itself rapidly and efficiently, in contrast to the divisions and dissensions that perturbed the enemy. Franco clearly took advantage of the execution by the republicans of the leader of the *Falange*, José Antonio Primo de Rivera, and of the presumed accidents that led to the death of two prestigious generals, Sanjuro and Mola. With no political parties in the way, without any need to account to anyone, unhindered by freedom of the press, and backed by a Church that viewed the war as a genuine 'crusade', the Francoist army could exercise violence without limits.

Completing the picture were imbalances due to the policies of the international powers of the moment. The *golpistas* immediately received essential help from Nazi Germany and Fascist Italy. In addition to important quantities of arms, Germany deployed the Condor Legion, while Italy dispatched the Volunteer Troops Corps. Franco's army also benefited from the presence of Portuguese and Irish Catholic soldiers. On the republican side the only important support came from the USSR, which provided limited and irregular aid. There were also the efforts of the international brigades, mostly made up of communists who sympathized with the USSR. Significantly, the liberal democracies, most prominently France, the UK, and the United States, elected to adopt a strict neutrality, leaving the republic to its fate. The United States, moreover, sold fuel to the Francoist side.

Summarizing the course of the war in its broadest terms, from the start the Francoist 'national' side controlled, though not without hard fighting, Galicia, Castilela and León, La Rioja, Navarra, the western half of Aragon, northern Extremadura, and the area that connects Cádiz to Seville, in addition, of course, to the Spanish protectorate in Morocco, the Canary Islands, Mallorca and Ibiza. Its military progress was characterized by successive conquests of territory. The first, vitally important, consisted in transferring the troops from Africa to the peninsula, occupying Seville and a good part of Extremadura – there was a bloody massacre in Badajoz on the way – then linking up with the army operating in Castile and León. The operation enabled a rapid approach to Madrid through Talavera and Toledo. In parallel, the republic failed to conquer Zaragoza and Huesca, which would have facilitated the fusion of the forces on the Cantabrian coast with those on the Mediterranean.

Franco's army invested a good part of its capabilities in an offensive on Toledo, which allowed the capital, Madrid, to prepare its defence; with the help of the international brigades, these gave the desired results. The Francoists were more successful in two other offensives. The first, between June and October 1937, led to the occupation of the Basque Country, Cantabria and Asturias, with the loss of considerable economic resources for the republic. Previously, in April of that same year, the infamous bombing of Guernica by the German Condor Legion had occurred. The second rebel offensive led to territorial gains in Andalusia, culminating in the bloody occupation of Malaga in February 1937.

Successive republican counter-offensives in Brunete, Belchite, and Teruel – the only provincial capital occupied, ephemerally, by the republican army – were unsuccessful. The Francoist offensive in Guadalajara in March 1937 also failed. In April of the following year, upon reaching the Mediterranean at Viñaros, Franco's army succeeded in dividing the territory controlled by the republic in two, and in separating Catalonia from the rest of that territory. The last republican effort of substance, also ending in defeat, was the battle of the Ebro, fought in the summer and autumn of 1938. Barcelona fell to Franco at the end of January 1939 – giving rise to a massive exodus – and Madrid was occupied at the end of March. Valencia, Alicante, and Cartagena were the last redoubts of the republic, where many refugees gathered, eager to find ships to transport them to France or North Africa.

It is often said that the victorious Francoist army staged a coup and waged a civil war in an effort to restore 'order' to a country in chaos. As if the word 'order' had a single, indisputable meaning, marking the Francoist project as an unequivocal good. By all evidence, however, there were multiple and very distinct perceptions of the meaning of 'order'. The Francoist order was rooted in the firm intention of preserving the position of the privileged classes in Spanish society. Among its main objectives, therefore, was the reassertion of exploitation in the factories, and to keep the land in the hands of the landed gentry.

Excesses and Violence

A common depiction of libertarian militants during the civil war, in particular during its first phase, associates them with endless acts of violence and terror. According to this depiction, spread by the propaganda machinery of the Franco regime, but also by supporters of the republican order, the libertarian world overflowed with criminals who, in addition to being responsible for 'common' crimes, carried out summary executions of right-wingers, the rich, and priests – some six thousand were assassinated during the war – and the burning down monasteries and churches with feverish abandon. Moreover, as regards their conduct, especially in Catalonia, the settling of accounts from the era of *pistolerismo* during the early 1920s played its part.

There is no sense in denying that in the weeks immediately following the coup there were acts of unbridled violence from the confederal ranks, violence whose roots lay in decades of lacerating inequalities and abuse. Certainly, there were also opportunists who took advantage of the situation. The latter were undoubtedly joined by the 'common' prisoners who had been freed on July 20 in Barcelona (it should be emphasized that in the libertarian world the classification of prisoners as 'political', 'social', or 'common' was rejected). Although the CNT was the organization best suited to act as cover for criminal activity – the one that exercised the least control over its militants – members of other political forces and unions were also involved in violence to a significant degree. Furthermore, in the confederal world there were militants bravely dedicated to the task of saving lives. Such was the case of Melchor Rodríguez, nicknamed the 'red angel', who, as a prison delegate in Madrid, put an end to the mass executions of prisoners, so infamous in the initial months of the war.

The excesses of the anarchist world were in any case incomparably less than those that occurred during the fascist coup, in which extreme violence, meticulously planned and professionally executed, was employed against the most oppressed and penalised layers of Spanish society. And they were also fewer than those that, in later months, were carried out by the repressive apparatus of a republic increasingly policed by the PCE and its allies, willing to emulate the spasms of violence manifested in Stalin's USSR.

Mujeres Libres

Mujeres Libres [Free Women] was an organization whose activity ran from the spring of 1936 up to the end of the civil war. It encompassed 150 groups and incorporated some 20,000 members, among whom the work of militants such as Amparo Poch, Mercedes Comaposada, and Lucía Sánchez Saornil was noteworthy. The movement was clearly the precursor to what today is described as anarcho-feminism.

In the libertarian world of the 1930s, feminism was commonly seen as a bourgeois discourse and practice, closely related to suffragism, that championed specific legal reforms of little interest to anarchist women. The latter were of course in favour of equality between women and men in labour and social rights. They denounced the lower salaries earned by women, rejected the double exploitation they suffered, and emphasized the negative effects of the limited female presence in the educational system. But anarchist women went further, contesting patriarchal society and male authoritarianism as a whole. In this regard they confronted three modes of enslavement: women's relative lack of education, their inferior social status, and their exploitation as workers. Although anarchist women occasionally defended the institution of the family, at other times they chose to support free and equal love. Many of the views of *Mujeres Libres* were manifested in their commitments to the collective education of children, the socialization of domestic work, the so-called *liberatorios de prostitución* [support services for prostitutes], ambitious programmes to open nurseries, and care for war refugees.

Mujeres Libres advocated for the creation of specifically female organizations in the libertarian world. These organizations were needed because, as far as women were concerned, and despite Federica Montseyn's affirmation that 'anarchism has never established distinctions between man and woman', major problems persisted. 'I have seen many homes, not only of simple confederates, but of anarchists (?!), governed by the purest feudal norms,' wrote Lucía Sánchez Saornil in an article. A text from January 1937 noted that 'music halls and houses of prostitution are still filled with red and red/black scarves, and all kinds of anti-fascist insignia'. It was often emphasized that confederal organs operated on the assumption that women were not able to play prominent roles, or that to do so they required the help of men. Also, during the civil war, it was not uncommon for collectives to pay men more than women. Perhaps certain views found in the libertarian world of the 19th century had yet to be overcome – those that took women's role to be exclusively limited to the home, and that when she accessed the job market, she only fostered the misery and degradation of workers by taking jobs away from men. And this despite the undeniable fact that successive congresses of the CNT explicitly advocated for the right of women to work towards their economic independence.

Mujeres Libres had every reason to challenge a notion very widespread in libertarian organizations: that of the revolutionary ideal as a man brimming with masculine attributes, in contrast to the weak condition of women, condemned to play a minor role. In fact, despite the efforts made, that notion persisted throughout the civil war, when women – for the first time wearing trousers and with short hair – were eventually ordered away from the frontlines.

The foregoing did not prevent women from enjoying a broad experience of liberation between 1936 and 1939, having gained greater economic and sexual freedom, and freedom of movement. As such, regardless of the problems affecting anarchist organizations, it is difficult to imagine that *Mujeres Libres* could have emerged from anywhere other than the CNT. Its leading members, dedicated to teaching, writing, and unionizing, were clearly aware that the social revolution would not in itself end many of the burdens affecting women, who were in need of an emancipation that demanded a revolution of its own.

The Agrarian Collectives

The first and arguably most important signal of the social revolution to which we have referred was the collectivization of agriculture. It took place above all in Aragón where, according to one estimate, it affected 70% of land not controlled by the Francoist side, with some 300,000 people involved. But processes of collectivization also occurred in Catalonia, Valencia, Murcia, and La Mancha and, more ephemerally or less consistently, in some parts of Andalusia and Extremadura.

It is difficult to address the agrarian collectives in a measured and thorough manner, since in practice they were quite varied. They arose, moreover, in conditions as complex as they were conflictual, indelibly marked by the proximity to the frontline, the pressures of the war, and by the manifest hostility of part of the population. The protagonists were overwhelmingly peasants, frequently illiterate but endowed with common sense, a spirit of self-sacrifice, and a willingness to cooperate. They had no use for the collaboration, and even less for the direction, of specialists and intellectuals. Along with militants of the libertarian organizations there was also a strong presence of members of the socialist UGT, almost always against the directives of the union's central leadership. Also involved were many peasants who were, according to the widespread saying, 'anarchists without knowing it'. The words of George Orwell describe the scenario well: 'the Spanish working class did not, as we might conceivably do in England, resist Franco in the name of "democracy" and the *status quo*; their resistance was accompanied by – one might almost say it consisted of – a definite revolutionary outbreak.

Land was seized by the peasants; many factories and most of the transport were seized by the trade unions.'

The collectivization of agriculture was to a large extent an application of the concept of libertarian communism outlined at the Congress of Zaragoza in May 1936. 'Once the violent aspect of the revolution is over, these are abolished: private property, the State, the principle of authority, and consequently, the classes that divide men into exploiters and exploited, oppressed and oppressors. Once wealth is socialized, organizations of producers, now free, will be in charge of the direct administration of production and consumption.' In many of its manifestations it constituted a new system, distinct from the municipalities of the time and from the unions themselves. It might perhaps have approximated the model of medieval councils. In the opinion of the anarchist doctor Isaac Puente: 'libertarian communism is the organization of society without the State and without individual property. For this there is no need to invent anything, nor to create a new organism. The nuclei of organization, around which future economic life will be organized, are already present in today's society: they are the Union and the Free Municipality.'

Collectivists were deeply aware of the limitations of policies designed to merely nationalize the economic system. 'What proceeds is socialization, and to socialize is, in clear and forceful terms, to hand over the property, hand over the production, to the professional unions,' stated an article published in *Fragua Social* [Social Force] in November 1936. The term 'expropriation' was not used, as it had a negative dimension and said nothing about the final destination of what was expropriated, which could well have been an illiberal state-bureaucratic apparatus. Although collectivization took many forms, underlying them all was a model of organization that had been imagined thousands of times by local peasants. It fused a utopian communism rooted in deeply-established traditions, an echo of the libertarian ideal, an acute sense of solidarity, and responses to the imperatives of the moment, which amplified historical pressures that had never been resolved.

We noted that collectivization took on different forms. In all cases there was some sort of forced expropriation, whether executed locally and autonomously by landless peasants, who in most cases were militants of the CNT or UGT, or, such as in Aragón, by libertarian militias arriving from Catalonia. There were of course episodes of violence against rich landowners and those seen as sympathetic to the military coup. The right of smallholders to continue working their land was generally respected, though attempts were usually made to convince them to join the collectivizing wave. These small owners certainly feared that their properties would be taken by force and knew that without machinery and means of transport they would find themselves in a delicate situation. In many cases smallholders were allowed to participate in local assemblies, with the understanding that they were prevented from owning more land than they could cultivate and were required to not disturb the general order. Where smallholders were in the majority, collectivization barely gained any ground. Notably, both the PCE and the *Partit Socialista Unificat de Catalunya* (PSUC; United Socialist Party of Catalonia) – product of the fusion of four small socialist and communist parties in Catalonia – made a show of defending the rights of smallholders.

Both work and consumption were usually administered according to collective criteria, a practice that was stimulated by the urgency of carrying out agricultural work at a time when many men were leaving for the front. Where private property was abolished, efforts were made to open collective canteens, schools – often installed in abandoned monasteries – printing presses, laboratories for agricultural experiments, and cinemas. The principle of mutual aid was applied, for example in the pooling of tools and the adoption of radical formulae of wage equalization. Local currencies were in many cases established. 'Here in Fraga one can throw one thousand peseta bills into the street and nobody will pay attention. Rockerfeller, if you came to Fraga with your entire bank account, you wouldn't even be able to buy a cup of coffee. Money, your god and servant, has been abolished here, and the people are happy,' read a libertarian newspaper. Efforts were made to coordinate and federate the collectives on a regional basis. The most successful was the so-called *Consejo de Aragón* [Council of Aragon], initially exclusively libertarian and later opened up to people of other political orientations.

Naturally, none of this means there were no problems. As noted, there were unjustifiable acts of violence, though far fewer than those carried out by the Francoist rebels. And there was some egotistical behaviour and theft, along with the persistence of unequal salaries for men and women – according to one estimate, the salaries were equal in only half of the collectives – and controversies about who should be the 'owner' of the land: the unions, the collectives themselves, or the revolutionary committees of the first moment. Moreover, peasants frequently took advantage of the circumstances to rid themselves of debt.

We have already noted that collectivization was not limited to Aragón. In the Valencian Country and in Murcia, where republican institutions continued to exercise control to a degree not seen in Aragón, there were collectivist projects of incontestable efficacy, specifically regarding the export of citrus fruits. At the start of 1938 some five hundred collectives incorporated 130,000 people. In Catalonia, according to a perhaps exaggerated estimate, three hundred collectives were formed, with 70,000 members. In Madrid and La Mancha, where the collaboration with the UGT was very close, the collectives numbered 230, and in 1937 had 100,000 people. Adding developments in Andalusia – with 63,000 involved, in Extremadura – with 6,000, and, more ephemerally, on the Cantabrian coast – with 13,000; the collectivization of the fishing industry in Gijon and Laredo was particularly important; according to Frank Mintz, one should speak of 758,000 collectivists in agriculture, to which we must add 1,080,000 people in industry, mostly Catalan: a total of 1,838,000 people. Other estimates, however, speak of three million, including family members.

It is not easy to assess the results of the collectivist experience.

Differing evaluations owe much to their own ideological lenses, and fair judgments are infrequent, while laudatory defence and easy demonizations, both weighed down by their ideologies, are common. It is perhaps best to compare the outcomes of collectivist efforts to the enormous failure of the attempts at agrarian reform carried out by successive republican governments between 1931 and 1936. The common view in the libertarian world was that large landowners, finding themselves under little pressure from the government, were entirely unwilling to accept such a reform, which, moreover, would have only been another cog in the engine of capital and the State. It seems we can conclude, however cautiously, that the balance sheet of collectivization was more than favourable, all the more so if the difficulties of the time and the obstacles imposed by the bureaucracy and State institutions are taken into account. Suffice it to recall the surprise of the Count of Romanones on finding significant improvements to his lands in Miralcampo and Azuqueca, in Guadalajara, upon regaining possession. The phenomenon was repeated in industry, when in 1939 factory owners discovered that their enterprises were evidently in better shape than three years earlier.

One should not, in any case, assess only the strictly economic results: we must also observe the radical transformation in human relations brought about by the viewpoint of mutual aid. A publication of the FAI emphasized that collective work banishes hatred, envy, and selfishness, opening the way 'to a sense of solidarity and of mutual respect, since all who live in the collective, and of the collective, must be treated as a vast family'. The fact that individual liberties were preserved, under very difficult conditions, must be highlighted. The very resolution on libertarian communism approved by the confederal congress of May 1936 spoke of the need to guarantee individual sovereignty. Let us add that many collectives welcomed numerous refugees, above all from Madrid, and supplied food to towns near the frontline.

The Council of Aragón was dissolved in August 1937 by the

republican government of Negrín, with the assistance of an army division headed by the communist leader Enrique Líster. The arrest of libertarian militants was accompanied by their expulsion from municipal councils and by the dissolution of many agrarian collectives. The restitution of properties to those who had lost them in the summer of 1936 was in many cases enforced. These measures, clearly harmful to agricultural performance, were criticized even by militants of the PCE. Even so, the majority of collectives survived until the arrival of the Francoist army, and continued to welcome new members: evidence of the firm loyalty of many peasants, and that the collectivist project was more efficient and useful than its detractors have recognised.

The Collectivization of Industry

In addition to affecting the countryside, processes of collectivisation also occurred in urban areas, impacting many enterprises. They did so mainly in Catalonia, where, according to one estimate, 75% of the country's industry was located. These collectivization efforts were again the product of decades of activism by the libertarian world, and of the existence of organizations that came together in, above all, the CNT. Despite this, they had a largely spontaneous character, in that instead of obeying instructions from above, they were determined by the autonomous decisions of ensembles of workers. Industrial collectives demonstrated that workers could run companies efficiently on their own: they knew the processes of production and distribution perfectly, and directed their efforts at advancing them, while company profits now went to workers' wages. The collectivization of industry was a glaring demonstration of the possibility and benefit of dispensing with bosses, and proved that the social division of labour was not a fact of nature.

Conditions in the industrial world were more complex than in the countryside. There was the war, and with that the severing of commercial links to markets that supplied or purchased goods; the unwillingness of the republican authorities to dispense economic and financial assistance; the flight of many technical specialists; the disdain and open opposition manifested by many leftist political parties; the hostility of the ruling classes, in Spain and abroad; the political drift of the officials of the CNT and the FAI, quite clearly committed, as we shall see, to an uncritical insertion into republican institutions; and, finally, the absence of an active international movement of solidarity.

Collectives formed in industry, in commerce, services, and notably in transportation. A few days after 18 July 1936, the metros, trams, and buses in Barcelona were operating normally. Services such as water, electricity, telephone, and gas had also been socialized, while luxury hotels were converted into eateries for the people. Bakeries, for their part, immediately guaranteed the supply of bread. Within weeks a military industry, which Catalonia lacked, began to emerge through a process of reconversion that gave good results. According to one estimate, collectivization affected 70% to 80% of companies, and led to the creation of conglomerates within each economic sector. Although the UGT was very weak in Catalonia, many of its militants actively participated in the collectives.

Banking, however, was not collectivized, largely because the UGT dominated the sector. Some believe that had it been otherwise, there would have been greater and more effective financial support for industry and services, and the whole system would have succeeded. There were also difficulties with foreign financial companies, which in many cases escaped collectivization and became isolated, making it difficult to address the financial crisis in a holistic manner. Beyond Barcelona, the later nationalization of transportation gave the republican authorities very significant powers of obstruction and control, which no doubt had negative effects on many local collectives, agrarian and industrial.

Among other difficulties, there was some tension between a pressure to increase salaries and to shorten the working day versus the demands of the war. Despite the desire for everyone to have a job, wage differences between worker categories were greater than in the agrarian collectives. Certain self-serving practices began to emerge in some more or less privileged sectors, which as a result were subjected to greater union control. For the most part the appearance of unjustifiable competition between collectivized enterprises was dealt with efficiently by the threat of sanctions.

Many collectivized companies expressly set out to reduce, if not erase, differences in salaries across job roles, and to use the resulting savings to develop health care services, provide subsidies to the unemployed, guarantee a decent life in case of illness, pregnancy, or accident, and care for the elderly – who carried out many important duties – and the disabled. Many initiatives were launched that aimed at lowering the prices of essential goods, increasing the quality of products, improving the state of public health and hygiene – six hospitals and 37 health centres were opened in Catalonia – to develop consumer cooperatives, to reduce rents, and to bolster the training of workers.

The *Generalitat de Catalunya*, the autonomous government, enjoyed some success when, under the decree of collectivization and worker control of October 1936, and with the collaboration of the leadership of the CNT, it consolidated government control over many factories. The decree effectively meant that republicans, socialists, and communists re-established their leadership over the factories, to the detriment of credible practices of self-management, though in practice it had little relevance and workers went on as they had before its promulgation. The text of the decree contemplated the collectivization of companies of more than a hundred workers and those whose employers had been declared fascist or had fled. Meanwhile, smaller companies could be collectivized if there was an agreement to that effect between workers and owners, or if three quarters of the former so decided. The *Generalitat* reserved for itself powers of supervision and control which it was often in no condition to exercise.

The offensive against the collectives after May 1937 (we shall return to this) seems to have resulted in a decline in their performance. Many workers, demoralized, appeared to be profoundly dissatisfied, in particular once the arms industry was nationalized. But the decline was not limited to the defence industry; also affected were many industries in which workers confronted a statizing and bureaucratizing force that sought to replace workers' capacity for autonomous decision-making with politicians, bureaucrats, and functionaries. Despite this, as with many agrarian collectives in Aragón, a significant fraction of the collectivized industries continued to function as such until the occupation of Catalonia by the Francoist troops.

Beyond Self-management: Ecology and Growth

In the summer of 1936, when the greater part of the Catalan industry was collectivized, there was little debate about which goods should be produced. With the exception of enterprises undergoing conversion to arms production, the outputs remained mostly unchanged, though, of course, they were produced in a self-managed way. It is certainly true that the imperatives of the war left no room for deliberations that in other circumstances would have been of decisive importance, such as those related to economic growth, the use of scarce resources, choices of technology, and threats to the environment.

Nevertheless, and unlike elsewhere, many workers in the Spanish libertarian world proudly rejected the slavery of factory and field, and paid close attention to the great debates over freedom and the dignity of work. On occasion they expressed the firm conviction that, sooner or later, the revolution would bring about a reduction of the working day, and often attributed greater importance to leisure and culture than to salaries. Labour strikes out of solidarity with prisoners often aroused more enthusiasm than those that were strictly about wages.

Murray Bookchin suggests that many workers in the cities on the Spanish Mediterranean coast conserved a living memory of a non-capitalist culture, resisting the control exercised by clocks, factory whistles, foremen, machines, and opposed to the atomizing vortex of large cities. He adds that if in Spain there was a class approximating a 'German proletariat', its members were more oriented towards the UGT and the Catholic trade unions than libertarian organizations. There were workers who clearly perceived the effects of industrial production on the environment, on workers' health, and on the creation of socially and ecologically unnecessary goods. 'But man, not knowing how to recognize true happiness, wants to correct nature, reduce it; it is because of this human error, because of senseless marvels, that this indulgent earth has been transformed into an immense ossuary and is trampled in its greatest depths; the raw materials needed for its subordination are extracted, gathered into pestilential conglomerates. The mountains are stripped of their sombre green diadem, the rivers diverted from their course, the forests depopulated,' read a text by Alfred Marné printed in *La Revista Blanca*. Some libertarians rejected the view, which was so Marxist, according to which the impact of authoritarian factory culture was actually healthy, as it enabled the formation of a disciplined and united proletariat. There was a clear consciousness of the fact that the economy served the interests of a few.

Significantly, the document on libertarian communism approved by the CNT congress of May 1936 identified as outliers those communes that, 'refractory to industrialization', and linked to naturism and nudism, were unable to satisfy all their needs and would therefore be forced to strike agreements with conventional agricultural and industrial communes. Such an assumption, while perhaps correct, also masked a possibly ill-founded supposition that these 'irregular communes' could not become self-sufficient. This assumption was consistent with the delicate effort, evident in 1936, to unify processes of production by closing many small factories, in keeping with a centralizing mentality of dubious economic and social rationality. And with the imposition, by the very CNT – though of course not only the CNT – of a productivist logic that during the civil war clashed with forms of rejection of work, such as absenteeism, non-compliance with schedules, work-to-rule actions and slowdowns, the faking of illnesses, theft of goods, sabotage, and general indiscipline. A case in point was the struggle by many workers to maintain the observance of religious holidays. Against such indiscipline, and for reasons that were hardly trivial, the authorities brandished the needs of the war and the consequent pressure to increase productivity, both of which made many workers feel uneasy: they had made a revolution just to work more than before.

Anarchists in the Government

If there is one issue that, even today, continues to arouse heated debates in the Spanish and international libertarian world, it is the decision taken by the CNT-FAI in the autumn of 1936 to participate in the republican government. Although there are libertarians who say they understand the situation was delicate and options were limited, today the decision is commonly seen as unfortunate – embraced, moreover, by a leadership that failed to consult the rank and file. A good part of the latter, by all evidence, was oriented toward building a new society, and had little interest in the goings-on among the elite. It was in any case tragic that within a libertarian organization the decisions of the leadership diverged from the wishes and actions of those at the base.

The CNT initially advocated a sort of federation of local entities, free of states and parties, and an alliance with the socialist UGT. Such notions were soon dropped, however, and the CNT opted to participate in efforts to rebuild the institutions of the state. Not only that, it promoted the dissolution of popular militias not under its control, a stop to collectivist initiatives, and a visible erosion of local power. Many anarchists were thus complicit in a project that clearly valued victory in war over the cost of halting the revolution.

The first step in this process – quite distinct from the process initiated by the already-mentioned *Consejo de Aragón* – occurred in Catalonia, where libertarians accepted the disappearance of the initial *Comité Central de Milicias Antifascistas* (Central Committee of Anti-Fascist militias) and soon, in September 1936, merged

Federica Montseny (1905-1994

with the government of the *Generalitat*. At the beginning of November, in a second stage, four representatives of the CNT – Juan García Oliver, Juan López, Federica Montseny, and Joan Peiró – joined the Spanish republican government led by the socialist Francisco Largo Caballero, taking over the ministerial portfolios of, respectively, justice, commerce, health, and industry, which remained in their hands until May 1937. The presence of García Oliver and of Montseny, figures linked to the FAI, was particularly striking.

The arguments employed to justify participation in the Catalan and Spanish governments are well-known: to guarantee the supply of weapons and financing, to prevent others from taking advantage of policies and enactments, to collaborate with other anti-fascist forces – before imposing a model of their own – and to prioritise victory in war above all other considerations. Some see positive aspects, with respect to strongly felt social and moral demands over how the ministries were administered. Suffice it to recall the legislation in matters of abortion, adoption, common-law couples, and prison life that were associated with Federica Montseny, the first woman in Spain to direct a ministry. And yet, it seems that none of the objectives that justified participation in the governments were ever achieved – something that was finally recognized by many of the *cenetistas* who supported the process.

While it is of course easy to judge after the fact, the reality was that there were no palpable improvements in the military and financial situations. Nor was there progress regarding the non-intervention policy of countries like France, the UK, and the United States. There was little if any effect on the defence of the collectivizing revolution. It seems paradoxical that the CNT leadership was often criticized by the republican authorities and by the PCE, when in fact their collaboration was, unhappily, obvious and loyal: rather, unity was betrayed by others. The best indication of failure, in the end, is that both the revolution and the war were lost.

Let us end on the assessment given by two libertarian

thinkers. The first, Vernon Richards, highlighted the effect of the denaturing of the CNT:

> The strength of the CNT lay in its uncompromising opposition to the state and political intrigue; in its decentralized structure and in its opposition to the universal practice of paid and permanent officials; in its concern with the objectives of workers' control of the means of production as the necessary step towards libertarian communism, while at the same time courageously putting forward the immediate demands of the toiling masses for better working conditions and a recognition of their elementary freedoms.

The second, Emma Goldman, affirmed the following:

> I am deeply persuaded, very sure, that if the CNT-FAI, having everything in its hands and under its control, had blocked the banks, dissolved and eliminated assault guards and civil guards, put a lock on the Generalitat rather than collaborating with and joining it, given a mortal blow to the entire old bureaucracy, swept away adversaries near and far – today, you can be sure, we would not suffer from the situation that humiliates and hurts us, because the revolution would have had its logical development to consolidate itself.

The Events of May 1937

The events of May 1937 in Barcelona were the main sequel to the militarization that had taken place over the previous months on the republican side. A militarization that in many cases, in the libertarian world, had been rejected due to profound misgivings, not the least of which was that many officers in the popular army sympathized with the Francoists. On the republican side the reason given was that militarization was the only way weapons could be distributed to all anti-fascist groups, reversing the discrimination suffered by the units of the CNT-FAI and of the *Partido Obrero de Unificación Marxista* [POUM; Workers' Party of Marxist Unification], a non-Stalinist communist force. The militarization revealed the dubious capabilities of many of the cadres designated by the authorities, in which political proximity was clearly rewarded over military capacity. The units that resisted this process, already underequipped, stopped receiving weaponry altogether.

In May 1937 a clash occurred in Barcelona between militants of the CNT-FAI and the POUM on one side, and military units linked to the PSUC on the other. The spark that ignited the conflict was an attempt to occupy the Telefónicas building, actually instigated by the PSUC and by the *Esquerra Republicana de Catalunya* [ERC; Republican Left of Catalonia]. The attempt was a result of both the growing prestige of Stalin's USSR in the republic, and the alliance between Spanish communists and the forces of the republican bourgeoisie. The 'events of May' led to a new capitulation by the CNT in favour of an increasingly fictitious anti-fascist unity, and support for the new government led by Negrín. This was accompanied by a very weak response to the repressive policies that, with the backing of that government, were carried out by the PCE and the PSUC. Sébastien Faure explained what happened in the following terms: 'I am not unaware that it is not always possible to do what needs to be done; but I know that there are things that it is absolutely necessary to never do.'

In the following months the CNT leadership accepted the nationalization of large industrial enterprises and the preservation of the private ownership of small businesses and commerce. This was so despite its apparent numerical strength – in the spring of 1937 the confederation had more than two million members, and the FAI had 150,000 at the end of the year. And despite the merger, in September 1937, of the CNT, the FAI, and the *Juventudes Libertarias* [Libertarian Youth] to constitute the so-called *Movimento Libertario de España* [Libertarian Movement of Spain]. Catalan institutions also visibly lost ground, victims of policies intended to convert them into mere local agents of the central power. In other words, the 'events of May' were the culmination of the CNT's policy of collaboration. After leaving the Spanish government, the leaders of the CNT once again turned their backs on the spontaneous revolt of the workers, thus reaffirming their conduct over the preceding months. They placed a full stop on confederal leadership in the republican zone, to the advantage of the Communist Party which, supported by the USSR, became stronger, as witnessed by the ban on the POUM and the assassination of its top leader, Andreu Nin. No surprise then that what happened in Barcelona in May 1937, including the response of the CNT-FAI, provoked a visible disenchantment among libertarian militants. The ephemeral attempts to forge an alliance with the UGT arrived late and found little support. All that was asked of workers was resignation and discipline in the face of a war that was, without question, being lost.

Los Amigos de Durruti

There was no lack of criticism from the libertarian world of the CNT's collaboration with republican institutions. Among the critics was a group called *Los Amigos de Durruti* (The Friends of Durruti), founded in March 1937, mostly by militants of the Durruti Column – a confederal column that had deployed to Aragón and later to Madrid, in the summer and autumn of 1936 – who were opposed to the militarization of the CNT and critical of its participation in the Catalan and Spanish governments.

Los Amigos de Durruti, who played a very active role in the events of Barcelona of May 1937, exhibited, like the FAI in its moment, a certain vanguardist character, highlighting the fact that CNT, and in general the libertarian world, lacked a revolutionary programme worthy of the name. The group largely adopted Buenaventura Durruti's positions between July and November 1936 – the month of his death, in unclear conditions, on the Madrid front – revealed above all in a radio speech in which he rejected the militarization of the popular militants, and criticized what he took to be a disturbing bureaucratization of the CNT.

From the perspective of *Los Amigos de Durruti* – who were harshly repressed and banished from the CNT world – militarization entailed the abandonment of what until then had been a social-revolutionary war, now replaced by a conventional war in which the class element was diluted, along with the lamentable concentration of all decision-making, the disappearance of any control from the base, and the erasure of the voluntary character of the militias. Notably, the process of militarization had not emerged from within the logic of the confederal units, as significant CNT militants such as Cipriano Mera had proposed.

In a similar vein, the Italian anarchist Camillo Berneri, also assassinated in May 1937, argued that only a revolutionary war could defeat Franco, so that to halt the social revolution in effect handed the budding dictator victory in war. Berneri was in essence echoing a widely held idea that the force of victory was in large part rooted in the triumph of the social revolution, so that without the latter, the corresponding impulse was significantly reduced.

The PCE and the End of the War

The entire course of the Spanish civil war was marked by the very notable rise and influence of the *Partido Comunista de España*. While in February 1936 the PCE only had a few thousand members, during the course of the conflict it gathered support – in many cases it was a flood – which on occasion included sectors of the petty bourgeoisie and of the entrepreneurial class whose properties had been confiscated in the summer of that year. It is undeniable that many respectable anti-fascists joined the ranks of the PCE. The progressive strengthening of the PCE clearly benefited from the military aid that the USSR dispensed to the republic.

A party of order, discipline, and hierarchy, logically much more attractive to the middle classes than the libertarian organizations, the PCE at all times emphasized a discourse of national independence and resistance to the invader, which distanced it from the demand for a social revolution. It strove to give the republic a patina of respectability that might bring foreign powers such as France and the UK to its side, and simultaneously remained submissive to the interests of the USSR. It was arguably the actions of the PCE, a party that, despite its rhetoric, actively sought to sow division among the anti-fascist forces, that derailed the formation of a common front against Francoism.

We have noted that the PCE unhesitatingly backed the interests of small entrepreneurs and peasants. One of the party's organs, *Frente Rojo* [Red Front] affirmed that 'under the reign of the extinguished, infamous *Consejo de Aragón*, neither the citizens nor property had the slightest guarantee'. Although the PCE recognized the expropriation of land belonging to those who had openly collaborated with the military coup, it rejected that of the large landowners who had not done so. Beginning in May 1937, the PCE restored private commerce, particularly in Catalonia, through the PSUC. Opposed to the collectivization of agriculture and industry, the PCE offered a regime of order, contrasting with the distorted and propagandistic image of other political forces that it disseminated, in particular against the anarchists. For the PCE, in short, no revolution whatsoever had occurred in the Aragonese countryside or in Catalan industry.

The strategy pursued by the leadership of the Communist Party of Spain during the civil war was rooted in its desire to rid itself of the POUM and to weaken the CNT-FAI. This policy gained ground during Negrín's government, which from May 1937 ensured that the overwhelming majority of important military posts were in the hands of the PCE. The same occurred in the political-repressive apparatus, in the so-called *Servicio de Información Militar* (Military Information Service), and in various agencies in the Ministry of Defence. With these tools the PCE fulfilled all its objectives, except for victory in war: it destroyed the POUM, split the Socialist Party, neutralized the Catalan nationalists and nullified the bulk of the CNT-FAI and its capacity for action. This is an interesting tribute to the cause of unity and revolution, the more so since the military benefits derived from the operation were less than obvious. A report from the Republican army concluded, with irony, that in the eyes of the CNT the soldiers close to the PCE were much better at conquering defenceless positions located in the rear than fortified locations on the front.

It became increasingly difficult for the CNT to maintain its collaboration with the Negrín government under such conditions. The government had proved incapable of halting Franco's military successes, yet doubled down on propaganda that suggested, against all evidence, that it was prepared to resist to the end. The PCE, which surely knew that the war was lost, strove by means of yet another spasm of manipulation to ensure that responsibility for the defeat would fall on the shoulders of others.

In March 1939, the increasingly untenable position of the republic led to the creation of the *Consejo Nacional de Defensa* [National Defence Council], supported by the CNT. It was no longer a matter of making revolution, but of avoiding the establishment, on the republican side, of a dictatorship that would destroy the fragile democracy and autonomous regime still existing in Catalonia. The creation of the *Consejo* caused the dismissal of Negrín and triggered intense fighting in Madrid between members of the PCE and *cenetistas*. The militant base of the CNT was once again not consulted on many of these measures.

The honourable peace that the *Consejo* hoped to achieve never came about: Franco refused to accept any of the conditions set for it, and without mercy occupied the capital at the end of March 1939.

The Franco Regime

The Franco regime emerged from an extremely bloody civil war and the acute repression that followed it. It carried out numerous executions and practiced torture habitually. Hundreds of thousands of people passed through prisons and concentration camps, while slave labour was employed in pharaonic works such as the *Valle de los Caídos* [Valley of the Fallen] and the Guadalquivir canal. The repression was forcefully extended to women, and many children were taken from their parents.

In its first years the Francoist regime imitated Hitler's Germany and Mussolini's Italy. It even actively collaborated with them, as evidenced by the fact that, despite formally keeping Spain out of the Second World War, it decided to send the so-called *División Azul* [Blue Division] to Russia to fight shoulder to shoulder with the German army. Despite dire omens, the regime survived the defeat of Germany and Italy in the war. Shortly after, in the 1950s, it received considerable support from the United States, which was interested in maintaining a fiercely anti-communist ally – the cold war suited Francoism well – and from 1953 the US military enjoyed the use of the military bases at Morón, Rota, Torrejón, and Zaragoza. The external relations of Francoism entered a path of relative normalization after the incorporation of Spain into the United Nations in 1955. Moreover, the regime disposed of the last remnants of the colonial empire. The major milestones occurred in 1956 –- when Spain granted independence to the northern Morocco protectorate, 1968 – with the independence of Equatorial Guinea, and 1975 – when Spain abandoned the western Sahara to its fate, whereupon it was immediately occupied by the Moroccan army.

During its forty years, Francoism held up the image of an untouchable head of state to whom it assigned a charisma that by all evidence he lacked. Though the harshness of the regime softened somewhat over time, its fundamental features did not change: the proscription of political parties, trade unions, and social organizations; the absence of rights and liberties; the farce of holding elections and referendums that were anything but free; and the persistent use of a hyper-controlled media, of censorship, and of permanent ideological indoctrination. The enormous weight of an omnipresent Spanish nationalism resulted in a permanent aggression against the 'nationalisms of the periphery' – Catalan, Galician, and Basque – that from the 1960s on encountered a violent response by a Basque armed organization, *Euskadi Ta Askatasuna* (ETA), which in 1973, during the last throes of Francoism, assassinated the head of government, Luis Carrero Blanco.

An extremely blinkered version of Catholicism was imposed, on a principle that was termed *nacional-catolicismo* [National Catholicism], in which the Church was in charge of the educational system, while coeducation was proscribed, homosexuality was condemned and punished, and the use of contraceptives was prohibited. The lacerating marginalization of women was particularly evident: condemned to work at home, women were subjected in all respects to the rule of their husbands. The ascendancy of the Opus Dei in the spheres of power during the 1960s contrasted with the appearance, in those same years, of an anti-establishment Church with its base in the people.

In the first decades of its existence, the regime, which had a fundamentally autarkic character, faced enormous economic problems. At the end of the 1950s a progressive liberalization began, which, in the context of the *Planes de Desarrollo* [Plans for Development], and with the help of tourism – increasingly buoyant and aggressive towards the environment – and of the arrival of foreign capital, enabled economic growth, a degree of industrial recovery, the appearance of an incipient middle class, and an increase in per capita income. The transfer of population from rural areas to the Basque Country, Catalonia, and Madrid, and in general to the cities, was complemented by important migratory flows, at first directed toward Latin America and later towards Europe. These developments notwithstanding, we cannot ignore the principal facts: by means of endless repressive mechanisms, Francoism at all times fostered a work environment that was manifestly favourable to employers, as evidenced by the denial of the right to strike and the prohibition of anything that smelled of free trade unionism.

Exile and Resistance to Francoism

The majority of refugees at the end of the civil war were probably *cenetistas*. The latter barely availed themselves, however, of escape networks used by others – for the most part routes to France, North Africa, and various American countries. Nor could they count on the support of affine political and trade union organizations in their host countries, unlike socialists and communists. This was all the more significant given the French authorities' harsh treatment of the refugees.

Many of those executed during the initial years of Francoism were *cenetistas*. According to one estimate, this was true of over 70% of those who suffered the death penalty in Barcelona. In the following years the libertarians were very active in illegal border crossing operations, enabling the removal of militants of all colours, and during the Second World War helping many French citizens who sought temporary refuge in theoretically neutral Spain. When France was liberated, anarchists constituted the largest group of exiles there – between 30,000 and 40,000. Many had been members of *La Nueve* (The Nine), an anti-fascist military unit that participated in the liberation of Paris in 1944, and whose slogan was significant: 'Our objective is not the Rhine, but the Ebro'. This desire never found satisfaction, however, since unfortunately the Franco regime did not collapse after the allied victory in 1945.

Because the 'influential militants' had either died, were in prison, or had been forced into exile, any relation with the base of the CNT by necessity collapsed. Two great conflicts emerged among the emigres. The first opposed militants in Spain to those in exile, mostly in France and Mexico; the second, more important, opposed supporters of collaboration with the republican governments [in exile] to militants hostile to it – some even proposed the creation of a Libertarian Party. As is easy to suppose, disagreements from the years of the republic and the civil war frequently resurfaced.

Part of the libertarian movement joined the maquis, guerrillas operating in mountainous areas of Spain – in Galicia, in Asturias, and León, in Cantabria, and in certain areas of La Mancha, Andalusia, and Valencia. Although at first the maquis organized by the PCE had greater prominence, when the latter decided to withdraw its support a libertarian guerrilla survived, led mainly by militants acting outside the CNT itself, and some communist guerrillas also continued to fight. The last anarchist maquis disappeared between 1949 and 1952, in Andalusia and Galicia. They were replaced by an urban guerrilla campaign, primarily in Catalonia, whose greatest representatives were Raúl Carballeira (who died in 1948), Josep Lluís Facerías, Quico Sabaté and Ramón Vila Capdevila 'Caraquemada', killed by the Francoist police in 1957, 1960, and 1963 respectively. There were also unsuccessful attempts to assassinate Franco, such as that by Francisco Granado and Joaquín Delgado in 1963; both were executed. During the 1970s, in the last throes of Francoism, there were again forms of urban guerrilla movements, including the *Movimiento Ibérico de Liberación* [MIL; Iberian Liberation Movement] and the *Grupos de Acción Revolucionaria Internacionalista* [GARI; Internationalist Revolutionary Action Groups]. A militant of the MIL, Salvador Puig Antich, was executed in 1974.

The CNT became progressively weaker in the sphere of workplace organizing, as demonstrated by its inability in the 1960s to respond to the appearance of the *Comisiones Obreras* [CCOO; Workers' Commissions], controlled by the Communist Party, which strove to exploit some of the legal means offered by Francoism. Although rejected by the bulk of the libertarian movement, there were at the time minor rapprochements between *cenetista* militants — those called *cincopuntistas* [five-points-ists] — and the regime's vertical unions, as the latter were eager to counteract the growing influx of the PCE in the factories. Still, it is undeniable that the libertarian world, dispersed and weakened, was not in the best of conditions in the last years of the Franco regime.

Reappearance After the Death of Franco

The death of the dictator, in November 1975, opened the way to a gradual liberalization of the regime, one of whose many effects was the legalization of the CNT in 1977. The CNT experienced a remarkable growth in the years immediately following its legalization. According to one estimate, in September 1977 the CNT had 130,000 members. Its symbolic force was well reflected in massive rallies such as those celebrated in San Sebastián de los Reyes (Madrid), in Valencia, and, above all, in Barcelona.

By leading major strikes, such as that of gasoline station workers, the CNT positioned itself in open opposition to the *Pactos de la Moncloa* [Moncloa pacts: the political agreements by which the Franco government devolved power to the new "democratic" regime] which, though agreed to by the CCOO and the UGT, and despite propaganda by the regime of the *transición*, required new sacrifices by workers already sufficiently castigated by the ignominies of Francoism. The risk that the CNT would continue to grow, and thus escape control of the emerging power, could well explain the so-called 'Scala events', a fire in a Barcelona nightclub in which four people died in January 1978. This was likely a police setup designed to place responsibility for what happened onto the CNT and libertarian organizations in general. The major effect was that the expansion of the main anarcho-syndicalist organization was interrupted, amidst the silence of the parliamentary left. The operation was completed by dividing up the assets of the union, further damaging libertarian organizations.

The early growth of the CNT was accompanied by sharp divisions, often along generational lines. These involved exiles who wanted to return to a militancy 'from the interior', versus younger members who were influenced by counter-cultural practices. The libertarian world, not just the CNT, seemed to equally attract segments of the old workers' militancy and a new generation that was in large part influenced by the French May of 1968. A wide variety of factions were active: anarchists, anarcho-syndicalists, *consejistas* – supporters of workers' councils – autonomists, situationists and, in time, environmentalists, feminists, and pacifists.

It was at times evident, however, that the situation after 1975 was very different from that before 1939. There had been a palpable loss of contact with society, in which an accommodating middle class was forcefully emerging. Francoism had succeeded in cutting the CNT's roots in factories and working-class neighbourhoods, and ended the culture and practices of self-management, which consequently encountered great difficulties in re-establishing themselves. While the libertarian world was unable to overcome the resulting challenges, both the social democratic and the Leninist left solved their own problems through a progressive acceptance of the rules of the game emerging from the 'regime of the *transición*', in which a compromise-oriented trade unionism was enthroned as the master formula for solving many social problems.

The Farce of Transition

It has often been suggested that the CNT was determined to permanently remain on the sidelines of history when it rejected the rules of the *transición política* [political transition] that began in Spain after Franco died in November 1975. As if the transition were such a rotund reality, yielding unquestionable results, so that no one in their right mind would refuse it. And yet, there were many reasons to oppose a process that has led directly to the many miseries of today.

First, it must be recognized that the concept of 'transition' is itself equivocal, as shown by the difficulty in determining its dates. Some view it as having ended in 1978, with the approval of the new constitution, while others extend it up to 1982, when the PSOE joined the Spanish government. Still others take it to be a process that in reality remains open. Whatever the case, after Franco's death an accord was forged by which some of the Francoist elites imposed their interests through the institution of the monarchy. This they did quietly, by wielding the threat of the military, which is why the status of guarantor of the unity of Spain is attributed to the armed forces. A key element of the agreement was the decision to apply a clean slate policy with regard to the crimes of Francoism. In Spain, unlike other places, there were neither trials nor convictions. Lawsuits had to be presented in Argentina, while some 100,000 *desaparecidos* were forgotten and two thousand mass graves remain unexhumed. In such a scenario it is hardly surprising that the *Partido Popular* [PP; Popular Party], leading the Spanish government as these lines are written, has successfully avoided condemning the coup of 1936 and the Francoist system from which it in fact proceeds.

The terms of the libertarian critique of liberal democracy are not difficult to enumerate. Liberal democracy is founded on lacerating inequalities and serves the purpose of ratifying them. The system constructs artificial majorities that distort, often in a dramatic manner, the true political commitments of the population. Formidable economic-financial corporations operate behind the scenes, and it is they who in the end determine the rules of the game. And this form of pseudo-democracy will not hesitate to use force when needed, as shown by the repression we see in our streets and the coups d'état in countries in the South that have the misfortune of owning desirable raw materials.

Unsurprisingly, all the aforementioned features are manifest in the self-proclaimed Spanish democracy of the last decades, which, if those were not enough, has acquired additional vices: the distribution of power between two large parties – PSOE and PP – whose political posture is substantially the same; an electoral system that is manifestly beneficial to these two political forces; widespread corruption; and 'revolving doors' that have strengthened the link between much of the political class and private economic interests. This panorama is completed by the leadership of two unions, the CCOO and the UGT, that customarily agree to unacceptable terms from employers; by a plethora of communication media bent on repeating the same drivel and engaged in the most abhorrent manipulations; and an institution, the monarchy, marked by corruption and the absence of transparency.

Spain gave birth to the so-called 'state of the autonomous communities'. Although the latter led to the enactment of decentralizing policies, breaking with the hyper-centralized unitary state characteristic of Francoism, the problems of the new structure are increasingly evident. ETA's violence, which survived well into the 21st century, was used on numerous occasions to justify ignoring the demands for greater autonomy, including the recognition of a right to self-determination. The course of events, following ETA's renunciation of armed struggle, first in the Basque Country in the form of the so-called 'Ibarretxe plan', and later in Catalonia, has confirmed that the Spanish constitution, grounded in an increasingly overt and essentialist nationalism of the state, is a padlock designed to block any process of secession. And this regardless of what popular support secession might enjoy.

As for the economy, it has by design preserved the bulk of the privileges of those who made huge profits under Franco and enabled new waves of businessmen and bankers. Here we see the effects of fiscal policy that seeks to consolidate the position of great fortunes under the pretence of 'national interests'. It is true that in this process, and especially between 1982 and 1996, there emerged the foundations of a meagre welfare state which, linked as it is to cheap petrol, has entered a visible crisis in recent years. The appearance of a welfare state cannot mask the policies of the successive socialist governments of Felipe González, which carried out the dirty work that the right wing did not dare accomplish overtly, such as weakening the unions, the virtual disappearance of local neighbourhood movements, and painful operations of industrial reconversion.

If, from a libertarian perspective, there is no reason to accept the credentials of liberal democracy, there is also no reason to accept those of a welfare state. These forms of economic and social organization belong exclusively to capitalism, drawing on the dying philosophy of social-democracy and compromise-oriented trade unionism. Welfare states make it unimaginably difficult to deploy forms of self-management from the base. They have not come to liberate – as they announced – the so many women who today are victims of a double or triple exploitation; they have no workable ecological solution; and, finally, they show no solidarity with the exploited and neglected inhabitants of the countries of the South.

Those who believed in the so-called 'Spanish miracle' have in recent times witnessed its disintegration, the bursting of the real estate bubble and of that genuine scam that is debt. The constitutional reform of 2011, executed in a rapid and semi-clandestine manner, laid bare the primacy of the interests of the banks and large enterprises, at the same time as it portrayed the situation of a European Union blatantly subordinated to those interests. The major result is an obvious rise in inequality and a significant increase in the percentage of the population situated below the poverty line, accompanied by increasingly disturbing environmental aggressions that compel us to question the whole mythology that continues to surround economic growth.

One of the most pathetic moments of the Spanish pseudo-democracy occurred in 1986, when the PSOE, then in power, changed course on the main military alliance of the capitalist world, by means of a manipulated referendum on the North Atlantic Treaty Organization (NATO). The pressure of the Western powers, and particularly that of the United States, produced its effects. It was aided by a powerful media apparatus determined to twist what was, with all evidence, a rejection of NATO by the majority of the population. The three decades that followed have been characterized by Spain's visible submission to North American dictates, and by another great myth, that of so-called 'humanitarian' interventionism. The incorporation of Spain in 1986 into what today is called the European Union also seemed to enjoy, by means of the mandatory exercise in manipulation, wide popular support, reinforced by the aid provided by Brussels in the form of structural and cohesion funds. As time passed the tables turned, in part because those funds were later significantly reduced, and in part because of the debt crisis, which was settled by active pressure by the EU on Spain to comply with what in fact was an immoral rescue programme. As a result, beginning in 2007 the popularity of the EU among Spaniards declined significantly.

Repression has always been present in the background of the 'regime of the transition'. It has entered a new phase in response to the appearance of the *movimento del 15 de mayo* [May 15 movement] in 2011, which denounced the general narrative of that regime. The passage of laws such as the so-called *ley mordaza* [gag rule], the invention of accusatory evidence, police infiltrations, the collusion of prosecutors and judges, and, finally, the practice of torture, have been, and are, since 1975, our daily bread.

The Libertarian Presence Today

Even though conditions in modern Spain cannot be compared to those before 1939, today Spain remains the country in which the libertarian world has its greatest presence. This can be attested by anarchists who, coming from the most diverse countries, encounter here a wide variety of unions, athenaeums, affinity groups, and social movements. It cannot be denied that openly anarchist organizations are much weaker than they were in the past, but anarchist ideas and their corresponding practices are nevertheless present in many places and take many different forms.

First of all, there are various syndicalist forces, the most important being the CNT, the *Confederación General del Trabajo* [CGT; General Confederation of Labour], and *Solidariedad Obrera* [Workers' Solidarity]. The CGT, which has the most members – some 80,000, according to one estimate – was the product of a split in the CNT and is more possibilist than the latter, as evidenced by the fact that it participates in union elections. Relations between the CNT and the UGT, very tense in the past, appear to have entered a calmer phase in recent years.

Secondly, there are many instances of recognizably libertarian practices, such as athenaeums and affinity groups, and, more recently, the growing number of anarchist book clubs. There is a myriad of self-managed social centres, some in squats, operating in a manner that can be understood as mostly libertarian. The same must be said of some ecovillages, of integrated cooperatives, and of the incipient movement of groups of workers who, operating as self-managed cooperatives, have taken control of companies on the brink of closure. It is striking, however, that even though workplace organizations remain the strongest forces in the libertarian world, their relationships with autonomous spaces such as these are in many cases slight.

We should also mention a myriad of initiatives that operate in a space that with some lightness of spirit we will term 'counterculture', manifested, for example, in comics, music, and publications of all kinds. The libertarian world is very close to social movements that draw upon pacifism, feminism, environmentalism, anti-globalization, de-growth, anti-developmentism, animalism, and the fight against repression. The very movement of May 15, (*15-M, movimiento de los indignados*) – horizontal, decentralized, assembly-based, and rejecting leadership and personalism – has drawn upon a libertarian current. The latter also inspires, in particular, the rise of anarcho-feminism and eco-feminism, which are committed to challenging those merely egalitarian projects based on a statist feminism that fail to address many of the key elements of patriarchal society.

These manifestations of the libertarian world, so disparate and so broad, speak of forms of social development that are not only not in the minority: they often enjoy authentic support in society, in powerful contrast with the image – that of a violent movement completely removed from the views of ordinary people – that the police apparatus and the system's means of (non-)communication are determined to project. That image is most often based on jarring manipulations, such as the arrest, surrounded by media attention, of libertarian activists, who after a time are freed without charge. But that intentionally distorted image is also contrary to the image of the old anarchists, those before 1936, retained by a significant part of the population. The latter looks with respect upon those who raised themselves above their material conditions, and who, with singular courage, challenged a lamentable and unjustifiable reality.

The Relevance of Anarchist Thought and Practices Today

Earlier in this book we left unanswered a question regarding the contemporary relevance of libertarian notions and practices. Many believe that anarchism is a withered world view, having irrefutably demonstrated its incapacity to face the challenges of complex societies such as ours.

In confronting this perception, we must first of all draw attention to the unflattering performance of three presumably alternative worldviews: the liberal, the social-democratic, and the Leninist. The first of these is today mired in an extreme form of short-term thinking – a victim of its own greed – as it persists in plundering the human and material resources of the planet. If any solution is contemplated for its enormous environmental problems, that solution is an eco-fascism that seeks to drastically reduce the planet's population. With respect to the social-democratic worldview, one must ask whether, in view of all that has occurred over the past decades, it is truly distinct from the liberal perspective. The age of cheap oil ended a long time ago, taking with it many of the foundations of that master project of social-democracy: the welfare state. As for Leninism, the collapse of Soviet-type systems laid bare the deficiencies of a project that was inherently authoritarian, hierarchical, anti-egalitarian, and deeply immersed in a veneration of productive forces.

Of course, the libertarian worldview does not magically solve any of the deficiencies and aberrations listed above. It nevertheless provides an exercise in lucidity that manifests itself in a great number of ways. Among these we have, first of all, the awareness that one must not confuse 'democracy' with 'liberal democracy', as our libertarians of the 1930s recognized when they rejected the mythical belief that the republic was, in itself, 'democracy'. Secondly, the libertarian perspective clarifies the kind of workplace organization that we actually need, necessarily linked to the nature of the contemporary society in which it operates, but also to the project of the future society. Because the reappearance of many of the labour conditions of yesteryear is almost certain, we can logically expect the rebirth of a more combative workplace organization. Third, the concept of 'propaganda of the deed' which attracted our attention in this text, acts as a basis for the creation of self-managed autonomous spaces, free from markets and patriarchies, which are evidence that things can be done differently than what the system we endure imposes upon us. Fourth, a suggestive discussion remains open around what 'education' should mean, demonstrated by proposals as disparate as self-managed public education, free and libertarian schools, or indeed the rejection of all projects of education, because they are manipulative and domesticating. As a fifth and last point, efficient solutions to problems that today seem unapproachable may well come from the South of the planet, in particular from what are sometimes called, with greater or less felicity, 'indigenous peoples'. Recent occurrences in Chiapas and Rojava, in the latter case at the hands of what is commonly described as 'democratic confederalism', give us some reasonable hope.

Beyond such issues, it is becoming increasingly evident that the prospect of a general collapse of the system gives new relevance to the libertarian project, as antidote to the collapse or as a response once it has occurred – once again, on the basis of self-organization, direct democracy and action, federalism, and mutual aid. The threat of collapse foregrounds verbs such as those that suggest we degrow, de-urbanize, de-technologize, de-patriarchalize, and de-complexify our societies, and forces an increasingly urgent discussion over the significance of economic growth, of supposedly liberating technologies, and welfare.

There is no reason to rule out the resurgence of libertarian movements as many-sided, adaptive, and combative as the CNT was a century ago. And we should be wary of the suggestion that, with the advent of industrialization and the consequent mass production and consumption, anarchism, burdened by its presumed lack of analytical rigor, lost touch with history. Those who – liberals, social-democrats, and Leninists – took over from the old anarchists, and many others, in directing the locomotive of history, have more than demonstrated their ineptitude.

Chronology

1868	Bakunin founds the International Alliance for Socialist Democracy. Fanelli visits Madrid and Barcelona.
1870	The *Federación Regional Española* (FRE) is established, affiliated with the International Workers' Association.
1871	The Paris Commune.
1872-1873	The Marx-Bakunin conflict within the First International.
1873-1874	The First Republic.
1874	The FRE is made illegal.
1879	Founding of the The *Partido Socialista Obrero Español* (PSOE).
1881	Emergence of the *Federación de Trabajadores de la Región Española* (FTRE).
1882	The *Mano Negra* events in Jerez.
1888	Creation of the *Unión General de Trabajadores* (UGT), a trade union linked to the Socialist Party.
1892	Hundreds of journeymen occupy the city of Jerez and demand a social revolution.
1893	Bombing of the *Liceo de Barcelona* theatre.
1896	Bombing of the Corpus Christi procession in Barcelona.
1897	An anarchist assassinates Cánovas del Castillo.
1898	Cuba and The Philippines declare their independence from Spain.
1906	Failed attempt on the life of king Alfonso XIII in Madrid.
1907	*Solidaridad Obrera* is established, in Barcelona.
1909	The *Semana Tragica* in Barcelona. Execution of Ferrer i Guardia.
1910	Founding of the *Confederación Nacional del Trabajo* (CNT).

1912	Assassination of Canelas, by an anarchist.
1914	Start of the First World War.
1917	Rapprochement between the CNT and the UGT. Bolshevik revolution in Russia.
1917-1923	Spread of the phenomenon known as *pistolerismo*.
1918	The CNT of Catalonia holds its congress in Sants.
1919	Strike at Canadiense. The CNT joins the Third International, on a provisional basis. The CNT holds a congress in Madrid.
1921	The *Partido Comunista de España* is established.
1923	Assassination of Salvador Seguí. The dictatorship of Primo de Rivera begins. First attacks by the anarchist group *Los Solidarios*.
1927	The *Federación Anarquista Ibérica* is constituted.
1930	End of the dictatorship of Primo de Rivera. Failed uprising against the monarchy in Jaca.
1931	Proclamation of the Second Republic. King Alfonso XIII goes into exile. Congress of the CNT in Madrid. Manifesto of *los Treinta*.
1932	Anarchist insurrection in the Alto Llobregat (Catalonia). Renters' strike in Barcelona.
1933	Events at Casas Viejas. Opposition syndicates are ejected from the CNT. The general elections are a triumph for the CEDA and the *Partido Radical*; start of the *bienio negro*. Anarchist insurrections in Aragon, La Rioja, Extremadura, Andalusia, Catalonia, and León.
1934	Revolution in Asturias.
1936	The *Frente Popular* wins the general elections. Events at Yeste. At its congress in Zaragoza the CNT approves a resolution on libertarian communism; the opposition syndicates re-join the Confederation. Coup d'état by the military. The civil war begins. Germany and Italy support the coup. Collectivization in the Aragonese countryside and in Catalan industry. The CNT joins the Catalan government. Franco becomes the leader of the rebels. The International Brigades deploy in

	support of the republic. With four ministers, the CNT enters the republican government. Battle of Madrid.
1937	Battles of Guadalajara, Brunete, Belchite, and Teruel. German bombing of Gernika. The "may events" pit the CNT and the *Partido Obrero de Unificacion Marxista* (POUM) against the *Partit Socialista Unificat de Catalunya* (PSUC) and the *Esquerra Republicana de Catalunya* (ERC). Camillo Berneri is assassinated. The CNT breaks with the Spanish government. The *Consejo de Aragón* is dissolved.
1938	Battle of the Ebro.
1939	Franco occupies Barcelona. Coup d'etat on the republican side, led by colonel Casado: the *Consejo Nacional de Defensa* is constituted. Franco occupies Madrid. End of the civil war. Many anti-francoists are forced into exile. Start of the Second World War.
1945	End of the Second World War.
1952	The last anarchist maquis disappear.
1953	Spain signs an agreement with the United States giving the latter access to various military bases.
1955	Spain joins the United Nations.
1957-1963	An urban guerrilla campaign is active, especially in Catalonia.
1963	Two anarchists, Granado and Delgado, unsuccessfully attempt to assassinate Franco.
1974	A militant belonging to the *Movimiento Ibérico de Liberación* (MIL) is executed in Barcelona.
1975	Death of General Franco.
1977	Legalization of the CNT.
1978	Events of La Scala.
1979	Emergence of a workplace organization that a decade later will call itself the *Confederación General del Trabajo* (CGT).
1986	Referendum on NATO. Spain becomes part of the European Union.

Suggestions for further reading: books and websites

For a wonderful book, full of interviews with participants, look at: Ronald Fraser, *Blood of Spain: An Oral History of the Spanish Civil War*, London: Pimlico, 1994.

The best available account of rebel women is by Martha A. Ackelsberg, *Free Women of Spain: Anarchism and the Struggle for the Emancipation of Women*, Edinburgh: AK Press, 2005.

For a study or urban life and conflict, look at: Christopher Ealham, *Anarchism and the City: Revolution and Counter-Revolution in Barcelona, 1898–1937*, Oakland: AK Press, 2010.

Those seeking an introduction to anarchist ideas worldwide might start with: Daniel Guérin, (ed), *No Gods, No Masters*, Edinburgh: AK Press, 2005. Also of interest: Joan Connelly Ullman, *The Tragic Week: A Study of Anti-clericalism in Spain*, 1875-1912, Harvard University Press, 1968.

Thoughtful surveys include: Julián Casanova, *Anarchism, the Republic and Civil War in Spain: 1931–1939*, London: Routledge, 2004 and Murray Bookchin, *The Spanish Anarchists*. Edinburgh: AK Press, 1997, begins with the earlier years and Jason Garner, *Goals and Means, Anarchism, Syndicalism, and Internationalism in the Origins of the Federación Anarquista Ibérica*, Edinburgh: AK Press, 2016, surveys the 1920s especially. On collectivization, see: Gaston Leval, *Collectives in the Spanish Revolution*, London: Freedom Press, 1975. Also useful: George Orwell, *Orwell on Spain*, Harmondsworth: Penguin, 2001.

Further books, many of them in Spanish, are listed in the bibliography below.

Websites in English

Freedom: *Spain and the World*, e.g.: https://freedomnews.org.uk/wp-content/uploads/2017/10/Spain-and-the-World-1937-01-22-Vol.-1-no.-04.pdf much is available online e.g. https://dds.crl.edu/item/320278; and https://mrc-catalogue.warwick.ac.uk/records/MSH/1/96
Kate Sharpeley Library: http://www.katesharpleylibrary.net
Lib Com: http://www.libcom.org

Websites in Spanish

Biblioteca Nacional de Espana http://www.bne.es/es/Catalogos/ BibliotecaDigitalHispanica/) e.g.: *Revista Blanca, La Tierra.*
http://hemerotecadigital.bne.es/issue.
vm?id=0026352842&search=&lang=es CNT (1938).
Cedall: *Solidaridad Obrera, Tierra y Libertad,* etc. http://www.cedall.org/
CGT, Spain: http://www.cgt.es
Mujeres Libres, https://cgt.org.es/revista-mujeres-libres/

CGT, Murcia http://www.cgtmurcia.org/cultura-libertaria/anarkobiblioteka/ Extentive library, indexed by author, title and theme.
CNT, Spain: www.cnt.es
Libre Pensamiento: http://librepensamiento.org/
Solidaridad Obrera: https://solidaridadobrera.cnt.cat/hemeroteca/

Bibliography

Aisa, Ferran, *La cultura anarquista a Catalunya*, Barcelona: Edicions de 1984, 2006.

Alberola, Octavio, Gransac, Ariane, *El anarquismo español y la acción revolucionaria (1961-1974)*, Barcelona: Virus Editorial, 2004.

Alvarez Junco, José, *La ideologia politica del anarquismo español (1868-1910)*, Madrid: Siglo veintiuno editores, 1976

Balcells, Albert, *Trabajo industrial y organización obrera en la Cataluña contemporánea, 1900-1936*, Barcelona: Editorial Laia, 1974.

Balcells, Albert, *El pistolerisme: Barcelona (1917-1923)*, Barcelona: Pòrtic, 2009.

Bar, Antonio, *La CNT en los años rojos: (del sindicalismo revolucionario al anarcosindicalismo, 1910-1926)*, Madrid: Akal, 1981.

Bécarud, Jean & Gilles Lapouge, *Los anarquistas españoles*, Barcelona: Laia, 1972.

Bernecker, Walther L., *Colectividades y Revolución Social*, Barcelona: Editorial Critica, 1982

Berneri, Camillo, *Guerra di Classe,* available online: https://app.box.com/s/kxlh2y36y3cuz0gg3vfg

Bolloten, Burnett, *The Spanish Revolution: The Left and the Struggle for Power during the Civil War*, University of North Carolina Press, 1979.

Brademas, John, *Revolution and Social Revolution: A Contribution to the History of the Anarcho-Syndicalist Movement in Spain: 1930-1937*, University of Oxford, 1953.

Brenan, Gerald, *The Spanish Labyrinth: An Account of the Social and Political Background of the Spanish Civil War*, Cambridge University Press, 2014.

Brey, Gérard, & Jacques Maurice, *Historia y leyenda de Casas Viejas*, Bilbao: Zero, 1976.

Buenacasa, Manuel, *El Movimiento Obrero Español, 1886-1926: historia y critica: figuras ejemplares que conocí*, Gijon: Jucar, 1977.

Calero, Juan Pablo (ed), *Anarquistas y marxistas en la Primera Internacional: un debate entre Francisco Tomas y Pablo Iglesias*, Palma de Mallorca: Calumnia, 2015.

Casanova, Julián, *Anarquismo y violencia política en la España del siglo XX*, Zaragoza: Institución Fernando el Católico, 2007.

Casanova, Julián, *Tierra y libertad: cien años de anarquismo en España*, Barcelona: Crítica, 2010.

Castells Durán, Antoni, *Desarrollo y significado del proceso estatizador en la experiencia colectivista catalana, 1936-1939*, Vigo: Nossa y Jara, 1996.

Christie, Stuart, *We, the Anarchists! A Study of the Iberian Anarchist Federation (FAI), 1927-1937*, Hastings: Meltzer Press, 2000.

Cleminson, Richard, *Anarquismo y sexualidad en España, 1900-1939*, UCA, Universidad de Cádiz, 2008.

Cruells, Manuel, *La revolta de 1936 a Barcelona*, Barcelona: Galba Edicions, 1976.

Díaz, Ignacio, *Asturias octubre 1934: la revolución sin jefes*, Muturreko Buratazioak, 2012.

Díaz del Moral, Juan, *Historia de las agitaciones campesinas anduluzas*, Madrid: Alianza Editorial, 1973.

Diez, Xavier, *Venjança de clase, Causes profundes de la violència revolucionària a Catalunya el 1936*, Barcelona: Virus, 2010.

Díez, Xavier, *L'anarquisme, fet diferencial català: influència i llegat de l'anarquisme en la història i la societat catalana contemporània*, Barcelona: Virus editorial, 2014.

Ealham, Chris, *Class, Culture and Conflict in Barcelona, 1898-1937*, Abingdon: Taylor & Francis, 2004.

Enzensberger, Hans Magnus, *Anarchy's Brief Summer: The Life and Death of Buenaventura Durruti: a Novel*, Kolkata: Seagull Books, 2018.

Folgare, Paul & Augustin Souchy, *Colectivizaciones: la obra constructiva de la revolución española : ensayos, documentos, reportajes*, Barcelona: Fontamara, 1977.

Gómez Casas, Juan, *Historia de la FAI: aproximación a la historia de la organización específica del anarquismo y sus antecedentes de la Alianza de la Democracia Socialista*, Madrid: Fundación Anselmo Lorenzo, 2002.

Gómez Casas, Juan, *Historia del anarcosindicalismo Español*, Gijon: La Malatesta, 2006.

Guillamón, Agustín, *The Friends of Durruti Group: 1937-1939*, Edinburgh: AK Press, 1996.
Guillamón, Agustín, *Ready for Revolution: The CNT Defense Committees in Barcelona, 1933-1938*, Edinburgh:: AK Press, 2014.
Herrerín López, Angel, *La CNT durante el franquismo: clandestinidad y exilio (1939-1975)*, Madrid: Siglo XXI de España, 2004.
Herrerín López, Angel, *Anarquía, dinamita y revolución social: violencia y represión en la España de entre siglos (1868-1909)*, Madrid: Los Libros de la Catarata, 2011.
Horowitz, Irving, *The Anarchists*, Abingdon: Taylor & Francis Group, 2018.
Íñiguez, Miguel, *Esbozo de una enciclopedia histórica del anarquismo Español*, Madrid: Fundación de Estudios Libertarios Anselmo Lorenzo, 2001.
Íñiguez, Miguel, *Enciclopedia del anarquismo ibérico*, Enciclopedia del anarquismo ibérico, Vitoria: Asociación Isaac Puente, 2018.
Kaplan, Temma, *Anarchists of Andalusia*, 1868-1903, Princeton University Press, 2015.
Lida, Clara E., *Anarquismo y revolución en la España del siglo XIX*, Madrid: Siglo Veintiuno de España, 1972.
López Sánchez, Pere, *Rastros de rostros en un prado rojo (y negro), Las casas baratas de Can Tunis en la revolución social*, Barcelona: Virus, 2014.
Lorenzo, César M., *Los anarquistas españoles y el poder: 1868-1969*, Paris: Ruedo ibérico, 1972.
Madrid, Francisco & Claudio Venza, *Antología documental del anarquismo español*, Madrid: Fundación de Estudios Libertarios Anselmo Lorenzo, 2001.
Marín Silvestre, Dolors, *Ministros anarquistas: la CNT en el gobierno de la II República (1936-1939)*, Barcelona: Debolsillo, 2005.
Marín Silvestre, Dolors, *Anarquistas: un siglo de movimiento libertario en España*,Barcelona: Ariel, 2010.
Marín Silvestre, Dolors, *Anarquismo: una introducción*, Barcelona: Ariel, 2014.
Masjuan Bracons, Eduard, *La ecología humana en el anarquismo ibérico: urbanismo "orgánico" o ecológico, neomalthusianismo y naturismo social*, Barcelona: Icaria, 2000.
Maurice, Jacques, *El Anarquismo andaluz: campesinos y sindicalistas, 1868-1936*, Barcelona: Editorial Crítica, 1990.
Meaker, Gerald H., *The Revolutionary Left in Spain, 1914-1923*, Stanford University Press, 1974.
Mintz, Frank., *Anarchism and Workers' Self-management in Revolutionary Spain*, Edinburgh: AK Press, 2013.
Monjo, Anna, *Militants: Democràcia i participació a la CNT als anys 30*, Barcelona: Laertes, 2003.

Morales Muñoz, Manuel, *Cultura e ideología en el anarquismo spañol, 1870-1910*, Centro de Ediciones de Diputación Provincial de Málaga, 2002.

Nash, Mary, *Mujeres libres*, Barcelona: Tusquets, 1976.

Navarro Navarro & Francisco Javier, *Los ateneos libertarios en España (1931-1939)*, Santander: La Neurosis o Las Barricadas, 2016.

Nicolás, Miquel & Miquel Amorós, *La revolución traicionada: la verdadera historia de Balius y Los amigos de Durruti*, Barcelona: Virus Editorial, 2003.

Núñez Florencio, Rafael, *El terrorismo anarquista, 1888-1909*, Madrid: Siglo veintiuno, 1983.

Olaya Morales, Francisco, *Historia del movimiento obrero spañol (1900-1936)*, Madrid: Confederación Sindical Solidaridad Obrera, 2006.

Oyón, José Luis & Vicente Casals Costa (eds), *Vida obrera en la Barcelona de entreguerras, 1918-1936*, Centre de Cultura Contemporània de Barcelona, 1998.

Paniagua, Javier, *La larga marcha hacia la anarquía: pensamiento y acción del movimiento libertario,*: Madrid: Síntesis, 2008.

Paz, Abel, *Durruti in the Spanish Revolution*, Edinburgh: AK Press, 2007.

Peirats, José, *The CNT in the Spanish Revolution*, (three volumes), Hastings: Meltzer Press/Christie Books, 2001-06.

Pérez Baró, Albert. *Trenta Mesos de Col·lectivisme a Catalunya, 1936-1939*, Barcelona:: Edicions Ariel, 1970.

Richards, Vernon, *Lessons of the Spanish Revolution, 1936-1939*, London: Freedom Press, 1953.

Rodrigo Mora, Félix, *Investigación sobre la II República Española, 1931-1936*, Madrid: Potlatch Ediciones, 2016.

Romero Maura, Joaquín, *La rosa de fuego: el obrerismo barcelonés de 1899 a 1909*, Barcelona: RBA, 2012.

Roselló, Josep Maria, *La vuelta a la naturaleza: el pensamiento naturista hispano, 1890-2000 : naturismo libertario, trofología, vegetarismo naturista, vegetarismo social y librecultura*, Barcelona: Virus, 2003.

Ruiz, Paula, *La mujer en el anarquismo Español*, Barcelona: Confederación General del Trabajo, 2017.

Santasusana Corzan, Marc, *Quan la CNT cridà independència*, Barcelona: Editorial Base, 2016.

Saña, Heleno, *La revolución libertaria: los anarquistas en la Guerra Civil Española*, Pamplona: Laetoli, 2010.

Seidman, Michael, *Republic of Egos: A Social History of the Spanish Civil War*, University of Wisconsin Press, 2002.

Seidman, Michael, *Workers Against Work: Labour in Paris and Barcelona during the Popular Fronts*, Berkeley: University of California Press, 1992.

Semprún Maura, Carlos, *Revolució i contrarevolució a Catalunya, (1936-1937)*, Barcelona: DOPESA, 1975.

Siguán Boehmer, Marisa, *Literatura popular libertaria: trece años de "la novela ideal" (1925-1938)*, Barcelona: Península, 1981.

Solà, Pere, *Francesc Ferrer i Guàrdia i l'escola moderna*, Barcelona: Curial, 1978.

Solà, Pere, *Las escuelas racionalistas en Cataluña, (1909-1939)*, Barcelona: Tusquets, 1976.

Tavera, Sunanna (ed), *El anarquismo español*, Asociación de Historia Contemporánea, 2002.

Termes, Josep, *Anarquismo y sindicalismo en España: la Primera Internacional, 1864-1881*, Barcelona: Crítica, 2000.

Termes, Josep, *Historia del anarquismo en España (1870-1980)*, Barcelona: RBA, 2011.

Tiana Ferrer, Alejandro, *Educación Libertaria Y Revolución Social*: España, 1936-1939, Madrid: U.N.E.D., 1987.

Tietz, Manfred & Bert Hofmann, *El anarquismo español y sus tradiciones culturales*, Madrid: Vervuert, 1995.

Uceda, Rubén, *El Corazón del Sueño: Verano y otoño de 1936*, Madrid: Confederación Sindical Solidaridad Obrera, 2014.

Ullman, Joan Connelly, *The Tragic Week: A Study of Anti-clericalism in Spain, 1875-1912*, Harvard University Press, 1968.

Vadillo Muñoz, Julián & Soledad Gustavo, *Abriendo brecha: los inicios de la lucha de las mujeres por su emancipación: el ejemplo de Soledad Gustavo*, Guadalajara: Volapük, 2013.

Vargas, Ricard, *Anarquisme i alliberament nacional*, Barcelona: Catarko, 2007.

Vega i Masana, Eulalia, *El Trentisme a Catalunya: Divergencies Ideologiques En La CNT (1930-1933)*, Barcelona: Curial, 1980.

Vicente, Laura, *Historia del anarquismo español*, Madrid: Los Libros de la Catarata, 2013.

Villar, Manuel, Emilio J., García Wiedemann & Juan Antonio Moya Corral, *El anarquismo en la insurrección de Asturias: la C.N.T. y la F.A.I. en octubre de 1934*, Madrid: Fundación de Estudios Libertarios 'Anselmo Lorenzo', 1994.

Various Authors, *El movimiento libertario español. Pasado, presente y future*, Paris: Ruedo Ibérico, 1974.

Various Authors, *La oposición libertaria al régimen de Franco, 1936-1975*, Madrid: Fundación Salvador Seguí, 1993.

Various Authors, *La muerte de la libertad: represión franquista al movimiento libertario*, Madrid: Confederación General del Trabajo, 2009.

Documentaries and Other Films

Berger, Lisa and Carol Mazer, directors,...*De toda la vida*,1984. 54 min.

CNT, *Archivo cinematográfico de la revolución Española,* CNT 1936-1939. CNT, 2012.

Colectivo Penta, *Quico Sabaté.* 1980. 27 min. https://archive.org/details/vimeo-15309582

Comas, Eulàlia, director, *Economia collectiva. L'última revolució de Europa.* 2014. 66 min. https://economiacollectiva.com/

Felipe, Juan, director, *Indomables. Una historia de Mujeres Libres.* Zer Ikusi/CGT Euskadi, 2011, 45 min.

Felipe, Juan, director, *El tiempo de las cerezas. 1977-1979. Eclosión libertaria.* Zer Ikusi/CGT Euskadi, 2015, 68 min.

Figueras, Valenti & Helena Sánchez, directors, *Vivir de pie. Las guerras de Cipriano Mera.* Los Sueños De La Hormiga Roja, 2009, 124 min.

Gamero, Juan, director, *Vivir la utopía.* La 2, 1997, 95 min.

García De Quirós, Antonio Jesús, director, *Memoria viva.* CNT - AIT, GuerrillART Colectiva, Malévola Films, 2014, 120 min.

Gomà, Lala; MONTANJÀ, Xavier (1996): *Granado y Delgado, un crimen legal.* La sept / Arte, Point du jour and Oviedo TV, 1997, 58 min.

Gómez, Manuel and Marco Potyomkin, directors, *Sueños colectivos.* Producciones Potyomkin, 2011, 104 min.

Loach, Ken, director, *Land and Freedom.* PolyGram Filmed Entertainment, 1995, 109 min.

Mateos Benito, Gonzalo, director, *Ingobernables, Un recorrido por la Cataluña anarquista del siglo XXI.* 2015. 97 min. https://www.youtube.com/watch?v=LdKD0nYhjas&t=1s

Ríos, Paco, director, *Durruti en la revolución española.* Christie Books, Fundación de Estudios Libertarios Anselmo Lorenzo, ARTIC Communicació, 1998, 57 min.

Rodriguez, Melchor, director, *El ángel rojo.* Argonauta Producciones, 2016, 84 min. http://documentales.org/documental/el-angel-rojo/

Vigil, Verónica and José María Almela, directors, *El cine libertario. Cuando las películas hacen historia.* Delta Films, 2010, 60 min.

Zer Ikusi, *Sara, una mujer de temple.* Zer Ikusi, 2010. 48 min.

Acronyms

15-M: *Movimiento del 15 de Mayo* (May 15 movement).
CCOO: *Comisiones Obreras* (Workers' Commissions).
CEDA: *Confederación Española de Derechas Autónomas* (Spanish Confederation of Autonomous Right-wing Groups).
CEDA: *Confederación Española de Derechas Autónomas* (Spanish Confederation of Autonomous Right-wing groups).
CENU: *Consejo de la Escuela Nueva Unificada* (Council of the New Unified School).
CGT: *Confederación General del Trabajo* (General Confederation of Labour).
CNT: *Confederación Nacional del Trabajo* (National Confederation of Labour).
ERC: *Esquerra Republicana de Catalunya* (Republican Left of Catalonia).
ETA: *Euskadi Ta Askatasuna* (Basque Homeland and Liberty).
EU: European Union.
FAI: *Federación Anarquista Ibérica* (Iberian Anarchist Federation).
FRE: *Federación Regional Española* (Spanish Regional Federation).
FTRE: *Federación de Trabajadores de la Región Española* (Federation of Workers of the Spanish Region).
GARI: *Grupos de Acción Revolucionaria Internacionalista* (Internationalist Revolutionary Action Groups).
IWA: *International Workingmen's Association* (International Workingmen's Association).
IWA-AIT: *Asociación Internacional de Trabajadores* (International Workers' Association).
MIL: *Movimiento Ibérico de Liberación* (Iberian Liberation Movement).
NATO: North Atlantic Treaty Organization.

PCE: *Partido Comunista de España* (Communist Party of Spain).

POUM: *Partido Obrero de Unificación Marxista* (Workers' Party of Marxist Unification).

PP: *Partido Popular* (Popular Party).

PSOE: *Partido Socialista Obrero Español* (Spanish Socialist Workers' Party)..

PSUC: *Partit Socialista Unificat de Catalunya* (Unified Socialist Party of Catalonia).

SIM: *Servicio de Información Militar* (Military Information Service).

UGT: *Unión General de Trabajadores* (General Union of Workers).

UHP: *Uníos, Hermanos Proletarios* (Unite, Proletarian Brothers).

USSR: Union of Soviet Socialist Republics.

Index

15-M (Movimiento de los Indignados), 141, 143
Abad de Santillán, Diego, 60
abolition of private ownership of land and water, 73
agrarian collectives, 102-106, 107-108, 112
agrarian economy in spain, 27
agrarian reform, 53, 57, 86, 107
Albacete, violent incident in Yeste, 87
alcohol, rejection of, 75
Alcoy insurrection, 32
Alfonso XIII, king, 51
Algeciras conference, 38
Alhucemas, military landing at, 49
Alianza Orbera, 83
alternative society, 73-75
Amigos de Durruti, Los, 123-124
anarchism: anti-militarism 20-21; anticlericalism in, 39; contemporary relevance of, 144-146; core ideas, 18-19; critique of patriarchal society, 20; defence of individual freedom, 21; definition and understanding, 17; in Andalusia, 34-35; in Catalonia, 34, 81; in Madrid, 34; in Malaga, 35; in Seville, 35; in Spain, 23-26, 34-35; in Valencia, 34; in the Spanish Civil War, 90-95; national question, 80-82; opposition to all forms of government, 55; opposition to capitalism, 19-20, 31; presence in modern Spain, 142-143; rejection of the state, 20; relationship with republicanism, 38, 55; schools and currents, 21-22; and the written word, 77-79
anarchist book clubs, 142
anarchist songbooks, 79
anarcho-collectivism, 22
anarcho-communism, 22
anarcho-feminism, 143
anarcho-individualism, 22
anarcho-syndicalism, 22, 43, 57
Andalusia: anarchism in, 34-35; emigration from, 27; insurrections in, 59; rebel offensive in, 96
anti-clericalism, 40, 75
anti-colonial policies, 82
anti-establishment church, 129
Aragon: council of, dissolution by Negrín's government, 107; insurrections in, 59
Ascaso, Francisco, 50, 59
Asturias: commune, 85; emigration from, 27; revolution of 1934, 53, 86, 87, 83
athenaeums, cultural centres, 70-72, 79, 142
athletics, 73
autonomies: Catalan, Basque, and Galician, 54, 137

Azaña, Manuel, role in the government of the popular front, 86

Bakunin, Mikhail, 17, 21, 31, 78
banks, 119, 140
Barcelona: defence committees of the CNT-FAI, 90; demolition of buildings in, 74; dockyards, murder of Francisco Ascaso, 90; events of May 1937, 121-122; fall to Franco, 96; growth of, 51; life expectancy in, 27; neighbourhood committees in, 70; nightclub fire (1978), 135; population growth in, 28; rent strike in, 1932, 71; Semana Trágica in, 20, 38
Basque country: banking in, 28; Euskadi Ta Askatasuna (ETA), 129; industry in, 28; population transfer to, 130; sympathetic movements in, 85
Berenguer, Dámaso, general, interregnum of, 50
Berneri, Camillo, 124
bienio negro, 53
bienio reformista, 53
birth control methods, 74
Blanco, Luis Carrero, assassination of, 129
Bolsheviks, 45, 47
Bookchin, Murray, 90, 113
Brennan, Gerald, 25

Cabet, Étienne, influence in Catalonia, 29, 40
Calvo Sotelo, José, assassination of, 87
Canadiense, strike at, 44
Canalejas, José, assassination of, 36
capitalism, critique of, 19-20, 31, 139

Carballeira, Raúl, 132
Carlist wars, 28
Casas Viejas, events in, 58
Castile and León, emigration from, 27
Castillo, José, assassination of, 87
Catalonia: aggression against nationalism, 129; anarchism in, 34; banking in, 28; collectivization of industry in, 109-112; emigration from, 27; independence of, 81; industry in, 28; insurrections in, 59; language and culture of, 81; separation from republican territory, 96
Catholic church: collaboration with government institutions, 39; influence in spain, 27
Charter of Amiens, 43
children, novel first names for, 75
cinema, commitment to, 79
Civil War, Spanish, 97-98, 99-101, 118-127
civil disobedience, 37
collectivization of agriculture, 35, 102-106, 107-108
collectivization of industry, 35, 109-112
colonialism, end of, 28
Comaposada, Mercedes, 99
Comisiones Obreras (COCO), emergence of, 132
Comité Central de Milicias, 91
Companys, Lluís, arrest of, 85
Confederación Española de Derechas Autónomas (CEDA), 53, 83
Confederación General del Trabajo (CGT), 142
Confederación Nacional de Trabajo (CNT): 18, 22, 37; assembly-based organization, 65; base and 'cupola' structure, 66-67;

cenetistas, exile and resistance of, 131; collaboration with republican institutions, 118-119, 123; counter-cultural practices, influence on younger members, 136, 143; criticism of, 123; founding of, 43; growth of, 43; growth after Franco's death, 135; in the Asturian revolt, 85; in the Spanish Civil War, 90-95; in the elections of February 1936, 86; in the military coup of July 1936, 88; involvement in neighbourhood committees, 70; involvement in robberies, 50; legalization of 1977, 135; membership, 68-69; membership in Third International, 45; militants, influential, 66-67; opposition to the Pactos de la Moncloa, 135; participation in Catalan and Spanish governments, 116, 118-119; programme of, 43; reappearance after Franco's death, 135; relationship with FAI, 60; relationship with PCE, 45; relationship with UGT, 44; return to legality, 50; role in elections, 53; role in events of May 1937, 121-122; role in everyday life, 70; unemployed, support for, 71; violence, support of, 47; weakening in workplace organizing, 132; workplace organization, 70
consejistas, emergence of, 136
Consejo Federal de la Región Española (CFRE), 80
Consejo Nacional de Defensa, 127
Consejo de la Escuela Nueva Unificada (CENU), 42
cooperatives, integrated, 142

Costa, Joaquín, 26
crisis of 1929, effects of, 51
cycling, 73
Cánovas de Castillo, Antonio, assassination of, 36

darwinism, defence of, 73
Dato, Eduardo, assassination of, 36
debt crisis, 140
decentralization, demands for, 54
degrowth, 145
Delgado, Joaquín, 132
democracy: direct, 18; Spanish, critique of pseudo-democracy, 138, 140
democratic confederalism, 145
direct action, 18, 35, 70
disease, prevention of, 74
División Azul, 128
Durruti column, 123
Durruti, Buenaventura, 50, 59, 67, 123
Díaz del Moral, Juan, 40

ecclesiastical property, confiscation of, 27
ecology and growth, 113-115
ecovillages, 142
education: debates about, in the libertarian world, 42; emancipatory pedagogy in Spain, 40; reduction in illiteracy, 57
elections: of 1931, 51, 53; of 1933, 53, 57: of 1936, 53, 86
emigration: to the Americas, 27; internal, 51, 130; to Latin America under Franco, 130
environmental aggressions, 140
Enzensberger, Hans Magnus, 90
Escuela Moderna: criticism of, 40; founding of, 38; influence of, 42
esperanto, study of, 75

Esquerra Republicana de Catalunya (ERC), 121
Extremadura, insurrections in, 59

Facerías, Josep Lluís, 132
Falange Española, 87, 94
Fanelli, Giuseppe, 31
faístas, conflict with *trentistas*, 63-64
Federación Anarquista ibérica (FAI): changes in, 60; establishment of, 59; in the republican government, 118; nature of, 60; role in insurrections, 59
Federación Regional Española (FRE), 31
Federación de Trabajadores de la Región Española (FTRE), 32
federalism, 17-18, 29; in the CNT, 44, 65; and the national question, 80-81; relevance today, 145
feminism, 20, 99, 143
Ferrer i Guàrdia, Francesc: execution of, 38; founding of the *Escuela Moderna*, 40
First International, 45
first world war, impact on Spain, 43, 45
Flórez Estrada, Alvaro, 19
Fourier, Charles, 29, 40
Franco regime: autarkic character of, 129; crimes of, 137; economic growth 130; economic problems under, 129; features of, 129; industrial recovery under, 130; initial years of, 131; order, 96; proscription of trade unions, 129; repressive mechanisms of, 130; resistance to, 131; softening over time, 129; women, marginalization of, 129; workers' rights, denial of, 130
Franco, Francisco: death of, 135; image of, 129; in the Spanish Civil War, 85, 88, 94
Francoist army, 94-95, 96, 108
free love, 73-74
freethinkers, 38

Galicia, emigration from, 27
Galán, Fermín, captain, 51
García Hernández, Angel, captain, 51
García Oliver, Juan, 50, 59, 60, 118
Generation of 1898, 28
Gil Robles, José María, 53
Goldman, Emma, 119
Granado, Francisco, 132
Grupos de Acción Revolucionaria Internacionalista (GARI), 132
Guardia Civil, 27, 58, 87
Guardia de Asalto, 58
Guernica, bombing of by Condor Legion, 96
guerrilla movements, 132
gymnastics, 73

hedonism, conflict with work ethic, 64
hiking, 73
Hobsbawm, Eric, 24-25
homosexuality, 74
Huesca, uprising in Jaca, 51
humanitarian interventionism, 140
hygiene, improvements in, 74

Ibáñez, Dolores, 65
Ibáñez, Félix Martí, 74
illiteracy: in Spain, 27; reduction in, 57
individual freedom, defense of, 21
inequality, rise in, 140
International Workingmen's Association (IWA), 31
Izquierda Republicana, 65

Jerez incidents, 35
jurados mixtos, 57
Juventudes Libertarias, 122

Kropotkin, Peter, 17, 19, 21, 78

La Rioja, insurrections in, 59
Largo Caballero, Francisco, 118
Lerroux, Alejandro, 53
ley de defensa de la república, 57
ley mordaza, 141
Layret, Francesc, assassination of, 47
libertarian calendar, 75
libertarian communism, 85, 91
libertarian municipalism, 80
libertarian practices, 142-146
libertarian thought, 17-22
libertarians: anticlericalism among, 39; conditions in last years of Franco regime, 133; exile and resistance to francoism, 131; involvement in robberies and murder, 47; party, proposed creation of, 132; presence in Spain today, 142; relationship with Bolshevism, 45; relationship with Republicans, 38
Líster, Enrique, 108
López, Juan, 63, 118
Lorenzo, Anselmo, 32
luddite practices, 29

Madrid: anarchism in, 34; demolition of buildings in, 74; fall to Franco, 96; growth of, 51; in the military coup of July 1936, 88; population growth in, 28

Malaga: anarchism in, 35; occupation by Franco, 96
Malatesta, Errico, 17
Mano Negra incidents, 35

Manuel Azaña, 53
Maquis, guerrillas, 132
Marné, Alfred, 114
Marx, Karl, 19, 31
masturbation, condemnation of, 74
Mera, Cipriano, 124
middle class, emergence of, 136
militarization, 121, 123-124
military coup of July 1936, 51, 57, 88, 91
military, Spanish: maintenance costs of, 28; role in spanish unity, 137
mining in Spain, 28
modernization efforts in Spain, 27
Mondragón, violent clashes in, 85
Montseny, Federica, 60, 118
Morocco: army, occupation of Western Sahara, 129; Spanish protectorate in, 38; war, 51
Morral, Mateo, 36
Movimiento Ibérico de Liberación (MIL), 132
Movimiento Libertario de España, 122
Mujeres Libres movement, 20, 82, 99-101
music, 79
mutual aid, 17, 19, 24, 26, 29, 73, 105, 107

nacional-catolicismo, 129
nationalism: aggression against, 129; Catalan, Galician, and Basque, 28; independence and sovereignty of non-State political entities, 81
naturism, 73
Negrín, Juan, republican government of, 107, 122
neighbourhood committees, 70-72
neo-malthusianism, 73
new urbanism, 73-74
nudism, 73

Opus Dei, 129
Orwell, George, 102

Pactos de la Moncloa, 135
pacifism, 37, 136, 143
Paris commune, 31
Partido Comunista de España (PCE), 45, 65, 125-127
Partido Obrero de Unificación Marxista (POUM), 121
Partido Popular (PP), 137
Partido Radical, 53
Partido Sindicalista, 63
Partido Socialista Obrero Español (PSOE), 32, 57, 65, 137, 140
Partit Socialista Unificat de Catalunya (PSUC), 121-122, 126
peasants, landless, 27
Peiró, Joan, 63, 118
Pestaña, Ángel, 45, 63, 68
Pi i Margall, Francesc, 29
pistolerismo, 47
Poch, Amparo, 99
police infiltrations, 36, 135, 141
political transition (transición política), 137
Popular Front, 53, 86
popular olympiad in Barcelona, 82
Prieto, Hóracio, 74
Prieto, Indalecio, 65
Primo de Rivera, José Antonio, execution of, 94
Primo de Rivera, Miguel, dictatorship of, 49
prisoners, liberation of, 60
proletarian culture, 70
propaganda of the deed, 37, 145
Proudhon, Pierre-Joseph, 17, 19, 21, 29
Puig Antich, Salvador, 132

rationalist schools, 42
real estate speculation, rejection of, 74
referendum on NATO, 140
repression, by government, 31,32, 35, 36, 57, 58, 71, 85, 141
republican left, 65
republican government (Second Republic), 51, 86, 91
republicans, 38, 51, 55
Revista Blanca, La, 78
revolutionary dictatorship, 91
revolutionary gymnastics, 59, 85
revolutionary transformation, 59
Richards, Vernon, 119
robbery and looting, 35
Rodríguez, Melchor, 98
Russian Revolution, 45

Sabaté, Quico, 132
Saint-Simon, Henri de, 29
Salvochea, Fermín, 32
Sánchez Saornil, Lucía, 99
Sanjurjo, José, 53, 94
Seguí, Salvador, assassination of, 47
self-managed autonomous spaces, 143, 145
self-managed cooperatives, 142
self-managed public education, 145
self-managed social centres, 142
self-management, 17, 18, 42, 68, 113
Semana Trágica, La, 21, 38
Seville, anarchism in, 35
sex education, 74
sexuality, contradictions in, 74
sindicatos de oposición, 63
social revolution, 35, 91, 93, 102-106
social theatre, 79
Solidaridad Obrera, 43, 142
sports activities, 73
Spanish Miracle, dissolution of 139

strikes, 29, 35, 37, 43, 44, 113, 135; general, 29, 43-44, 50
swimming, 73
syndicalism, 50, 60, 142

technology, contrasting opinions on, 19
Telefónica building, attempt to occupy, 121
tenant strike, advocacy for, 74
terrorism, anarchist, 36
Third International, 45
transition, to democracy, 135-137
trentismo 59; conflict with *faístas*, 63-64

unemployment, 51, 54, 57, 86, 111
Unión General de Trabajadores (UGT), 33, 44, 65, 91
urban working class, 70-72
Urbanística del Porvenir, La, 74
utopian socialists, 29

Valencia: anarchism in, 34; fall to Franco, 96; insurrections in, 59
vegetarianism, 73
Vila Capdevila, Ramón "*Caraquemada*", 132
voting rights of women, 53

welfare state, critique of, 139
work ethic, conflict with hedonism, 64; value and significance of, 18
workers' solidarity, 43
workers' self-management, 113-115
workers' choirs, 79
workers' control of the means of production, 119
workers' societies, 29
working conditions, struggle for better, 66
workplace organizations, relationship with autonomous spaces, 145, 143

Zaragoza, Congress of May 1936, 20, 37, 63, 87, 88